LIVING WELL WITH PERFECTIONISM

AN ADLERIAN JOURNEY TO SELF-ACCEPTANCE

Caroline Faifman & Lindsay Turner

COPYRIGHT © 2025
CAROLINE FAIFMAN & LINDSAY TURNER
ALL RIGHTS RESERVED.

Copyright 2025 Caroline Faifman & Lindsay Turner – All rights reserved
The content contained within this book may not be reproduced, duplicated, or transmitted without direct written permission from the authors or publisher.

Under no circumstances will any blame or legal responsibility be held against the publisher or authors for any damages, reputation, or monetary loss due to the information contained within this book, either directly or indirectly.

Legal Notice
This book is copyright-protected. It is for personal use only. You may not amend, distribute, sell, quote, or paraphrase any part of the content within this book without the consent of the authors or publisher.

Disclaimer Notice
Although the authors and publisher have made every effort to ensure that the information in this book was correct at press time, they do not assume and hereby disclaim any liability to any party for any loss, damage, or disruption caused by errors or omissions, whether such errors or omissions result from negligence, accident, or any other cause.

Cover Illustration Copyright © 2025 by Lindsay Turner.
Cover design by Lindsay Turner.
Book design and production by Marisha Kriel T/A Anthropology of Copy
Editing by Marisha Kriel T/A Anthropology of Copy & Jordana Frankel

ISBN: 979-8-9928967-0-1

DEDICATION

Caroline Faifman

I dedicate this book to the souls who have encouraged me and helped me in my darkest hours.

To my trusted therapists and mentors—Laurie Austin Nelson, Timothy Evans, and Buttercup Lawson Mayer—thank you for believing in me when I didn't believe in myself.

To my family: my parents, whose unwavering love and quiet strength have always anchored me; my husband, who inspires me to dream boldly; and my beautiful children, who are my greatest blessings and my wisest teachers. You remind me every day that love, not perfection, truly matters.

Lindsay M. Turner

I dedicate this book to my beautiful daughter, Raegan—the light of my life. You are my reason, my inspiration, and the one who gives me the courage to keep going when it feels impossible. I also dedicate this to my parents, who never stop believing in me and always remind me of who I am, even when I forget. And to my first baby, Kylie Sprinkles—my loyal, loving sidekick who has been by my side through every chapter of my adult life. You will always be part of my story.

CONTENTS

	Introduction	pg 1
Part I	**How Perfectionism Takes Hold**	**pg 14**
Chapter 1	The Perfectionist's Reflection	pg 15
Chapter 2	The Unseen Blueprint of Your Life	pg 26
Chapter 3	The Battle Between Who You Are and Who You Should Be	pg 39
Part II	**Where Perfectionism Begins**	**pg 47**
Chapter 4	The Perfectionist Child and The Roles We Play	pg 48
Chapter 5	Childhood Lessons That Shaped Your Standards	pg 63
Chapter 6	Chase the Impossible Dream	pg 78
Part III	**Challenge the Perfectionist Mind**	**pg 85**
Chapter 7	Rewrite Your Inner Narrative	pg 86
Chapter 8	From Inferiority to Self-Acceptance	pg 93
Chapter 9	The Power of Connection	pg 111
Part IV	**Build a Balanced Life**	**pg 123**
Chapter 10	Balance Work, Love, and Community	pg 124
Chapter 11	The Present Moment as Your Refuge from Perfectionism	pg 133
Chapter 12	Your New Best Friend, Your Inner Cheerleader	pg 142
Part V	**Embrace Imperfection and Resilience**	**pg 157**
Chapter 13	Dare to Be Imperfect	pg 158
Chapter 14	Failure as Your Greatest Teacher	pg 168
Chapter 15	The Art of Self-Acceptance	pg 181
	About the Authors	**pg 190**

INTRODUCTION

Embrace Imperfection Together: The Adlerian Guide to Perfectionism

This workbook is more than a guide—it's an invitation to step off the treadmill of never-enough, and into a space where your flaws aren't failures... They're judgement-free insights on the path to pursuing your goals and ambitions.

You're not alone in your perfectionism. And you don't have to overcome it by yourself either.

Inside, we blend humor, honesty, and powerful psychological insight with practical exercises to help you:
- Quiet the inner critic
- Stop comparing yourself to everyone else
- Release unrealistic standards
- And most of all—feel enough, exactly as you are

We wrote this workbook because we've lived through this struggle. We know what it's like to look like you have it together while quietly falling apart inside.

Imagine This...
It's 8:11 a.m.

You wake up later than you planned. For a moment, that familiar voice stirs—the one that wants to scold, judge, spiral. But today, you notice it...and choose not to follow. You take a breath and allow yourself to feel the difference those extra minutes made. No internal scolding. Just waking. Just beginning.

You brush your teeth without rushing. You pour your coffee. You sit quietly, without grabbing your phone or drafting the day in your head. No doom-scrolling. No mental whip. Just presence.

When you open your inbox and see it overflowing, your chest doesn't tighten. You answer what's urgent. You let the rest wait. You've learned you don't have to do it all at once to be worthy. You trust yourself. That's new. That's earned.

Mid-morning, a meeting. You speak up—your idea still a bit messy. You don't swallow it down like before. You let it live. It lands. The team doesn't need perfect. They need your perspective.

At lunch, you eat what sounds good, not what earns a gold star. You stop when you're full, not when the plate is clean. You don't enter it into an app. You don't shame yourself. You eat. You enjoy. You move on.

Later, you respond to that text you left unread for days. You apologize briefly, kindly. No overexplaining. No "I'm the worst" talk. You trust in the love that's there. You reconnect.

In the afternoon, you mess up. You forget something important. The old panic flares—but you catch it. You correct the mistake. You don't spiral. You breathe. You forgive.

At 6:00 p.m., you don't reach for "just one more thing." You close the laptop. You step outside. The light hits the trees in that way you love. A song from high school plays in your ears. You smile. You feel the air on your skin. You're here.

At night, you don't replay the day in mental court. You don't tally what you got "right." You read something beautiful. You fall asleep without promising that tomorrow you'll be "better."

You are already enough.

This book is not a map to become someone else.
It's a process of remembering who you already are.

Why We Use Adlerian Psychology

Perfectionism is not just a behavior; early experiences and feelings of inferiority profoundly shape it. Many traditional approaches, such as cognitive-behavioral therapy (CBT), focus on modifying behaviors or thought patterns, but they don't always explore the deeper reasons why we strive for perfection.

This workbook takes a different approach. Using Adlerian psychology, we explore the unspoken struggles behind the perfectionist mindset:
- Constant comparisons
- Unattainable standards
- Relentless self-criticism

By understanding why we strive for perfection, we can finally break free from the cycle.

Break the Cycle of Perfectionism
Alfred Adler's insights show us that perfectionism often comes from early life experiences that made us feel 'less than.' Striving for superiority is a subconscious way to compensate for that feeling.

But here's the truth:
- You don't need to prove yourself to be worthy.
- You don't need to be perfect to be enough.

By exploring the deeper 'why' behind perfectionism—instead of just managing its symptoms—you will be better equipped to grow, thrive, and create lasting change.

This is your invitation to embrace imperfection, let go of self-doubt, and step into the freedom of knowing: You were always enough.

Our Personal Journeys: From Perfectionism to Self-Acceptance
Before we dive in, we want to introduce ourselves—not as therapists who have it all figured out, but as people who have walked this road ourselves.

Caroline's Imperfect Story:
They say you shouldn't specialize in 'your thing,' but isn't that why most of us enter helping professions? My journey into therapy wasn't just a career choice; it was a calling born from my struggles with mental health.

From a young age, I grappled with anxiety and depression. Growing up in an affluent Connecticut suburb outside New York City, I felt the weight of a high-achieving environment. As I entered puberty earlier than my peers, I began to dislike my body and yearned to be someone different. It seemed everyone else was 'perfect,' free from the worries that plagued me. I felt inadequate, struggling to meet the lofty standards set by my surroundings.

This struggle led me to seek external validation, battling severe depression and anxiety. At 12, I started therapy and discovered yoga, though I couldn't imagine becoming an instructor then. Despite this early introduction to healing practices, my journey was far from smooth. Through my teens and early twenties, I faced eating disorders, addiction issues, relationship struggles, and self-harm.

The birth of my first child at 26 marked a turning point. Suddenly, I had a purpose larger than myself, shifting my focus away from my feelings of inferiority. This new chapter reinvigorated my quest for wellness, spurring me to explore ways to manage anxiety, build self-esteem, and better understand myself.

My battle with perfectionism has given me firsthand insight into its profound impact. If I were to analyze my own lifestyle, I'd say my core goals revolve around being loved, accepted, and—most fundamentally—not abandoned. This deep-seated fear of being alone has led me to strive to be indispensable, useful, and superior, hoping others would value and depend on me.

These strategies, however, often backfired. I found myself resentful of doing too much, struggling with superiority and inferiority complexes, and unable to see others as equals. Ironically, while craving connection and unconditional love, I set conditions for my self-love, believing that achieving a certain status would finally bring acceptance.

Even now, as I write this book, part of me believes its completion will unlock a new level of friendship, success, and acceptance. But I recognize this as another manifestation of my perfectionist tendencies—always chasing the next accomplishment, hoping it will quell my fears.

Throughout this journey, I've come to understand the complexities of perfectionism and its intersection with mental health. This understanding, along with my training in Adlerian psychology, yoga, and mindfulness, drives me to help others navigate similar issues.

I was initially drawn to Adlerian psychology for its holistic approach. As a yoga instructor interested in overall well-being, I resonated deeply with the idea of treating people as whole beings, considering their thoughts, feelings, behaviors, and social context. Adler's belief that physical health impacts psychological state (and vice versa) aligned perfectly with my experiences.

Adler's teachings helped me understand myself and make significant shifts in my life and relationships. I felt called to share this rich philosophy with you, hoping you'll reap similar benefits. This workbook comes to you from a lifetime on the path of wellness, filled with ups and downs, mistakes, and victories.

Being a therapist is not just a career but a lifestyle. When I worked in drug and alcohol rehabilitation, I was often asked if I was 'in recovery.' While I wouldn't say I'm in recovery in the traditional sense, I always answered that I'm in recovery from life. Mental health and healing are ongoing, never-ending journeys.

I don't believe we need to change ourselves fundamentally. Instead, we are perfect as we are, often requiring only the release of old thoughts and patterns that no longer serve us positively. It's like the song *"This Little Light of Mine"*—the light is already within us. We need to pull back the curtains, look around the shadows, and shield the flame from the wind so it can shine brighter and stronger.

Through my journey, I've learned that perfectionism is not about striving for excellence but about fearing inadequacy. By sharing my experiences and the tools I've gathered, I hope to guide you toward self-acceptance and a more fulfilling life. Remember, you're not alone on this path. Let's embark on this journey together, embracing our imperfections and discovering the strength that lies within them.
 — **Caroline**

Key takeaways from Caroline's journey:

- Perfectionism often stems from a deep-seated fear of not being 'enough.'
- Seeking external validation can lead to exhaustion and resentment.
- Self-acceptance means embracing the journey, not just chasing

the next milestone.

Lindsay's Imperfect Story
I had an unconventional companion from a young age—a DSM, the Diagnostic and Statistical Manual of Mental Disorders, not exactly the usual toddler's teddy bear. When I was about knee-high, my mom was embarking on her psychological journey of obtaining her PhD in psychology. She had this notion that diving into the complexities of the human mind was akin to playing detective by matching symptoms to DSM disorders. It was a game we frequently played together.

Under her guidance, with a DSM often in tow, I became the youngest pseudo-psychologist in the playground. I'd diagnose playmates, pets, and even inanimate objects with a genuineness only a child could exhibit. My mom would often say, 'Research is me-search,' instilling early on the idea that helping others frequently begins with understanding and addressing our challenges. With a cheerful *"Hello world, here I am,"* I embraced life with a fearless and sociable attitude. As the younger sister of someone with disabilities, I was often seen as the 'perfect' child, something that felt both flattering and suffocating. On the one hand, helping my sister navigate social situations was a source of pride. However, I also felt burdened by these expectations. It left me questioning whether I was living up to the 'perfect' social image or acting as an impostor, just performing a role that didn't fit me.

Like Caroline, I grew up under the towering expectations of New York City's elite circles, navigating through prestigious prep schools and constantly battling intense pressure to conform to an unrealistic standard of thinness. The demanding nature of this high-achieving environment was overwhelming. I experienced early puberty and consequently began to feel out of place among my peers. It often appeared that everyone else effortlessly embodied an ideal physicality that felt unattainable to my pubescent self. Comparisons led to a deep-seated sense of not being thin enough and struggling to live up to the 'modelesque' expectations surrounding body image.

Professionally, my dive into hospitality was driven by a passion for creating joy through meticulously planned events. It seemed like a natural progression of my social abilities. However, as I built my career around bringing people together, I often played the impromptu therapist, offering a listening ear and guidance amidst the festivities.

Combining my dual roles with deeply personal challenges, like losing my father and ending a ten-year abusive, narcissistic relationship, revealed a profound calling. These experiences inspired me to return to school and pursue a new path as a Licensed Mental Health Counselor. Interestingly, Caroline had recognized my natural therapeutic abilities long before I fully acknowledged them myself and encouraged me to lean into this potential.

But let's be real—my perfectionistic tendencies appear in every aspect of my life. I don't know about you, but for me, life often feels like a sitcom, with me as the protagonist caught in the relentless tyranny of 'shoulds.' I constantly wonder: What if I'd effortlessly achieved my ideal weight? What if I'd been brave enough to apply to my dream program at Newhouse instead of opting for the safer route at Syracuse University? What if I hadn't settled for a psychopathic, narcissistic partner and instead gone for gold, fearlessly pursuing my dreams without letting anything stop me along the way?

Even in everyday chaos, my perfectionism is right there, front and center. Take my signature dramatic entrances—arriving late, making an unintentional spectacle by knocking something over, and then taking an exaggerated bow to diffuse the tension. While it might be entertaining, this tendency reflects an Adlerian concept of perfectionistic procrastination: delaying action until conditions feel perfect, which, spoiler alert, they never are.

Despite the chaos, I've learned the importance of laughing at myself. My mom's saying, 'Research is me-search,' becomes more relevant daily. It's a reminder that the very struggles we try to hide often hold the most incredible wisdom, and in therapy, this is especially true. The best practitioners have frequently navigated their significant challenges, making them relatable, empathetic, and authentic.

My journey has taught me that perfectionism, while it promises control and success, often leaves you stuck in a loop of self-criticism and unmet expectations. For years, I let these tendencies dictate my life, striving for an unattainable ideal that only reinforced my feelings of inadequacy. Losing my father and escaping an abusive relationship were wake-up calls—proof that chasing 'perfect' can cost you time, energy, and joy.

I've also realized how perfectionism masks itself in the name of productivity or high standards. It whispers, *"If you can just get this one thing right, you'll finally be enough."* But in truth, pursuing flawlessness only fuels a more profound fear of being seen as imperfect. My struggles with weight, relationships, career choices, and self-image have taught me this the hard way.

Yet, these same struggles have shaped me. Through the ups and downs—from early challenges that shaped my sense of self, to creating hospitality events, to stepping into my role as a therapist—I've learned that our imperfections, vulnerabilities, and even our messiest moments are not just obstacles to overcome. They're the bridges that connect us to others. They help us build empathy, develop authenticity, and create a sense of belonging.

Today, I see perfectionism for what it truly is—a well-disguised barrier to living fully. True perfection doesn't come from achieving flawlessness; it comes from embracing our unique, imperfect stories and using them to further genuine connections and growth.

If my life feels like a sitcom sometimes, maybe that's the point. Perhaps the perfection is in showing up—late, messy, flawed—but willing to keep trying anyway.
—**Lindsay**

Key takeaways from Lindsay's journey:
- Perfectionism may disguise itself as ambition, productivity, or even humor.
- Unrealistic standards keep us stuck in cycles of self-criticism and doubt.
- True growth doesn't come from getting everything 'right.' It comes from showing up, flaws and all.

Introduction to Perfectionism and Adlerian Psychology
Perfectionism often hides behind the mask of achievement, convincing us that we must strive for more to be worthy. But this workbook isn't about changing you or making you 'better'—it's about helping you understand yourself, your thoughts, and your behaviors through the lens of Adlerian psychology. The goal? To help you cultivate self-acceptance, advance self-compassion, and build a sense of self-worth that isn't

dependent on endless achievements.

You are already deserving of love, kindness, and respect just as you are, regardless of your background, race, sexual orientation, or social status. There's no need to strive to become someone else, nor should you expect this workbook to magically 'fix' anything. Personal growth is a continuous journey, and there's no final destination. We're always learning about ourselves, our relationships, and our patterns. The focus is on letting go of what no longer serves you and finding new ways to navigate life with less emotional pain.

If perfectionism is something you struggle with, there's a good chance you're also dealing with anxiety and low self-esteem. This workbook will help you feel better and manage your perfectionist tendencies, not eliminate them. The great news is that you can remain a perfectionist while learning to use it to your advantage.

The Adlerian perspective provides a unique and insightful approach to understanding perfectionism, offering practical strategies for overcoming its challenges. More than a guide to perfectionism, this workbook is a path to understanding yourself, your relationships, and the world at a deeper level.

What is Adlerian Psychology?
Adlerian, or Individual Psychology, was founded by Austrian psychiatrist Alfred Adler in the late 19th century. Adler's approach focuses on understanding the whole person within their social context rather than just individual traits and behaviors. He introduced key concepts like inferiority, superiority, and our inherent drive to overcome feelings of inadequacy.

One of Adler's most important ideas is social interest, or our connection and concern for others, which he called 'community feeling.' Perfectionists often suffer from feelings of inferiority, which can grow into what Adler described as an inferiority complex. He distinguished between natural feelings of inferiority and the more destructive complex.

Everyone feels inadequate at times—that's normal. For example, you might think, *"I'm not a great cook, but I'd love to improve. I'll watch some tutorials and practice."* In this scenario, feelings of inferiority motivate you to grow and develop a skill. However, an inferiority complex arises when these feelings become overwhelming, triggering thoughts like, *"I'm a terrible cook, and I'll never be as good as others because I'm just not that talented. There's no hope for improvement. I'll never get better."*

This can result in a negative spiral of constant comparison, self-criticism, and the belief that you are inherently inferior. You might hear yourself thinking, *"I'll never measure up"* or *"I'm destined to fail."* In response, people with an inferiority complex may either give up on goals entirely or be overcompensated by pushing themselves to extreme measures to prove their worth. Perfectionism often arises from this need to overachieve to gain control, approval, and validation, even though perfection is ultimately impossible.

How Adlerian Psychology Can Help

Rather than merely addressing surface behaviors, it uncovers the deep-seated beliefs and patterns that fuel perfectionist tendencies, helping individuals develop healthier ways of thinking and relating to themselves and others.

In this workbook, you'll explore key Adlerian concepts that contribute to perfectionism, including:

- **Fictional Finalism** – The imagined or idealized goal we chase in the pursuit of perfection, often believing that reaching it will bring ultimate happiness or validation. However, these unrealistic standards usually lead to chronic dissatisfaction.
- **Lifestyle** – Your unique way of viewing yourself, others, and the world, shaped by early experiences. This personal framework dictates how you respond to challenges and influences your perfectionistic tendencies.
- **Family Constellation**—Your role within your family system subtly shapes your sense of identity and self-worth. Birth order, parental expectations, and sibling relationships all influence how perfectionistic tendencies develop.
- **Early Recollections** – The stories and memories from childhood that still influence your present self-concept and emotional responses. These recollections often reveal unconscious beliefs about success, failure, and self-worth.

Understanding these concepts allows you to recognize the underlying roots of perfectionism and begin to shift toward social interest—Adler's idea of contributing to and connecting with others in meaningful ways. Perfectionists often focus excessively on individual achievement, but true fulfillment comes from building relationships, creating a sense of belonging, and embracing imperfection as part of growth.

Move from Insight to Action
The goal of this section is not to change who you are but to provide tools for cultivating a healthier, more balanced life. Now that you've explored these key Adlerian principles, let's apply them through practical exercises designed to help you:
- Identify your fictional finalism and challenge unrealistic personal standards.
- Reflect on your lifestyle and how it shapes your perfectionist patterns.
- Analyze your family constellation to recognize early influences on your self-perception.
- Examine early recollections that might still drive your behavior today.

As we continue this journey, take a moment to reflect on how these core Adlerian principles have shaped your perfectionist tendencies. Approach this process with self-compassion and curiosity, not judgment. Growth isn't about achieving flawlessness; it's about understanding yourself more deeply and making intentional shifts toward a more balanced, fulfilling life. Living well with perfectionism is not about changing who you are but about freeing yourself from the beliefs and habits that no longer serve you.

Now, explore how these insights can help you rewrite your inner narrative and move toward greater self-acceptance and resilience.

Your Guide to This Journey: How This Book is Structured
This book is structured to take you on a step-by-step journey to understanding, challenging, and ultimately freeing yourself from the grips of perfectionism.

We have divided it into **five parts**, each designed to guide you through a different stage of self-exploration and growth.

Part I: Recognize the Patterns
- Identify how perfectionism shows up in your life
- Explore the hidden fears and motivations behind perfectionist tendencies

Part II: Unearth the Roots
- Understand where perfectionism comes from (family dynamics, childhood experiences, societal expectations)
- Recognize how your early experiences shaped your beliefs about success, failure, and self-worth

Part III: Challenge the Perfectionist Mind
- Learn to reframe thoughts and change limiting beliefs
- Develop a growth mindset that embraces mistakes and imperfection

Part IV: Build a Balanced Life
- Apply Adlerian psychology to create a more fulfilling, balanced approach to work, relationships, and self-care
- Explore social interests, self-compassion, and community connections

Part V: Embrace Imperfection and Resilience
- Cultivate self-acceptance, resilience, and adaptability
- Develop an ongoing recovery plan to sustain these changes

Each Chapter Includes
- Real-life case studies to make the concepts relatable
- Activities. exercises & journal prompts to help you apply the material to your own life
- Reflection moments to encourage deep thinking and awareness

How to Use This Workbook
This isn't a book to just *read*—it's a book to work through. You might find specific exercises challenging or uncomfortable, and that's okay.

Growth happens when we step outside our comfort zones.
1. To get the most out of this journey:
   Be honest with yourself. The more authentic you are about

your struggles, the more transformative this experience will be.
2. **Do the exercises.** Reflection and action go hand in hand—don't just absorb the information, apply it.
3. **Take your time.** Some chapters might hit close to home. Pause, breathe, and move at your own pace.
4. **Stay open.** The more open you are to shifting perspectives, the easier it will be to create lasting change.

PART I: HOW PERFECTIONISM TAKES HOLD

Before we can change perfectionism, we must first see it clearly. Perfectionists are often unaware of their deeply ingrained habits—how much they rely on achievement, approval, and control to feel worthy. Adler believed that our life patterns are not accidental but guided by the hidden beliefs we form in childhood.

In Part I, we explore the reflection of perfectionism and uncover the patterns that shape your life. Do you strive for growth or for approval? Are you driven by courage or by fear? Recognizing these patterns is the first step toward transformation.

Chapter 1: The Perfectionist's Reflection— The unconscious beliefs that shape perfectionism.

Chapter 2: The Unseen Blueprint of Your Life — Understanding the subconscious 'life script' you've been following.

Chapter 3: The Battle Between Who You Are and Who You Should Be— The internal struggle between your authentic and perfectionist selves.

CHAPTER 1: THE PERFECTIONIST'S REFLECTION

Perfectionism doesn't start with a goal — it starts with a fear.

Adlerian psychology teaches us that our beliefs about ourselves and the world are shaped early, often in response to feeling 'less than.'

The Perfectionism Trap

You have spent your entire life trying to be good enough. And yet, no matter how much you do or how hard you try, a part of you still whispers, *"Not enough."*

Many people struggle with perfectionism, yet few recognize the extent of its impact on their daily lives. Perfectionism often disguises itself as ambition, high standards, or the drive to be the best, making it appear productive and even desirable. However, beneath the polished surface, it often masks an invisible kind of suffering—one driven by self-doubt, fear of failure, and an unrelenting pressure to meet impossible expectations.

From an Adlerian psychology perspective, perfectionism is a coping mechanism for deep-seated feelings of inferiority. Perfectionists often believe that if they work hard enough, avoid mistakes, and meet external expectations, they will finally feel 'good enough.' Yet, that moment never comes. Instead, the bar moves higher, which creates a relentless cycle of frustration, burnout, and chronic self-criticism.

This chapter will examine how perfectionism manifests in your life and explore how Adlerian psychology explains the pursuit of an unattainable ideal. We will also introduce reflection activities designed to help you recognize perfectionist tendencies and understand their emotional impact.

The Perfect Client

When I meet a new client, I always ask them to fill out intake forms and answer questions about their goals for therapy. Recently, a client wrote:

"I want to gain my confidence and self-esteem back. I would like to find out how everyone else is so perfect here. What is it that I'm missing? When asked, everyone tells me I'm good, but I do not feel that way at all."

Does this sound familiar? It certainly did to me. As soon as I read these words, I knew I had found someone I could help.

Perfectionists often see themselves as inadequate compared to others, even when they receive praise or external validation. This is the perfectionism trap—the belief that everyone except you has it figured out. It's the idea that others are naturally confident, successful, and flawless, while you struggle to meet the exact expectations.

However, the truth is quite different: almost everyone battles with self-doubt at some point in their lives. The difference is not in reality but in perception—perfectionists magnify their flaws while idealizing others.

Pause for Reflection

Take a moment to reflect and answer these questions honestly. Don't worry about the 'perfect' answer. As we already discussed, there's no such thing. The goal is to notice where perfectionism might run the show in your life. Once you write this down and then step back and look at it, you can shift how you approach these moments.

1. **Where in your life do you feel the pressure to be perfect?**
   - Is it at work, in your relationships, or maybe in your appearance? Think about the areas where you always strive to meet an impossibly high standard.
2. **How does perfectionism show up in your day-to-day decisions?**
   - Are there tasks you put off because you fear they won't be good enough? Do you find yourself repeatedly redoing things, trying to get them just right?

3. **What's the cost of your perfectionism?**
   - Perfectionism often comes with a high price—whether it's your time, energy, or peace of mind. What have you given up in the pursuit to be flawless?

The Paradox of Self-Worth

Why is it so easy to tell others they are doing well, but so difficult to believe the same about ourselves?

Many perfectionists live by the *"I'll be happy when..."* mentality:
- *"I'll be happy when I lose weight."*
- *"I'll feel successful when I get promoted."*
- *"I'll feel confident when I'm finally good enough."*

But here's the problem—no achievement ever feels like enough.

Even after we reach a goal, a perfectionist's mind quickly shifts to the next challenge, instead of celebrating:

"Sure, I accomplished that... but I should have done it better."

This endless pursuit leaves anyone who struggles with perfectionism hollow—perfectionists are never truly at peace with themselves, always chasing an ideal that remains just out of reach.

Sound familiar?

Loved ones might tell us we're good parents, successful at work, or kind friends. Yet, we still feel 'not good enough.' This is the paradox of self-worth.

- We easily encourage others but find applying that same support toward ourselves challenging.
- We have been told all our lives to 'work on our self-esteem'—but how?
- How do we stop chasing an unattainable version of self-worth?

That's why we wrote this workbook.

After spending two decades studying Adlerian psychology, we have identified actionable, reliable steps to increase self-esteem and manage perfectionism. Through this book, we are eager to share these insights with you, including:

- The actionable steps to build self-esteem.
- How to end the *"I'll be happy when"* mentality.
- Providing answers to why we never feel 'good enough' to be worthy of happiness and love.

Defining Perfectionism

At the 2024 Florida Adlerian Society conference, a question was posed to the attendees: *"Who here is a perfectionist?"* The responses were fascinating. Several people raised their hands, some sought further clarification, while others hesitated, uncertain if they fit the definition. This reaction is typical among perfectionists, marked by concerns such as, *"What if I don't answer this correctly?"* or *"Am I a perfectionist only in certain aspects, and does that count?"* Such questions reflect their desire to provide the 'perfect' answer. A hallmark of perfectionism is the fear of making mistakes, often leading individuals to seek additional information for clarity or refrain from answering altogether.

While perfectionism affects everyone differently, societal expectations shape how men and women experience and express their pursuit of perfection.

For many women, it's a physical epidemic that manifests in our bodies. We drive ourselves to conform to societal beauty standards and fit a specific size. Motherhood also presents opportunities to pursue the ideal of being the perfect mother. However, when we inevitably fall short of this unrealistic goal, we are consumed by guilt. This guilt stems from our desire to please and our instinct to say yes to everything, so that we avoid disappointing others.

Men typically chase perfection through power, and that power tends to show up in some questionable ways. A big one? An obsession with sex. It often becomes less about intimacy and more about dominance, status, and the ability to prove something. It is almost as if masculinity and conquest become fused, psychologically and emotionally.

The drive for power doesn't stop at sex. It extends to material symbols, too—luxury cars, designer watches, and other status symbols. In my experience working with men, these pursuits aren't random. They're trying to measure up, and frequently believe that highly visible displays of wealth will earn them respect, admiration, and control. In other words, they're chasing the appearance of perfection.

What Is Perfectionism?

Perfectionism is not simply about *the need to do well*—it's about never feeling like you've done *enough*.

Adlerian psychology teaches us that perfectionism is born from a deep sense of inferiority. Adler believed everyone starts life feeling small and dependent, which drives them to strive for growth and mastery.

However, when unrealistic societal or familial expectations distort this natural striving, it becomes an incessant need for flawlessness.

Perfectionists often believe:
- *"If I don't get it right, I'm a failure."*
- *"Mistakes mean I'm not good enough."*
- *"If I relax, I'll fall behind."*

Instead of striving for excellence with self-compassion, perfectionists chase an impossible standard, fearing that they will never be worthy without perfection.

The Illusion of Perfection

As Adler once said, *"The only normal people are the ones you don't know very well."* If that's true, it makes you wonder—does the same apply to 'perfect people'? Are they real, or are we chasing an unrealistic mirage? The idea of perfection is often built from a distance.

We scroll through social media, see the 'perfectly' put-together family down the street, or hear about a friend of a friend who seems to have it all. From afar, it's easy to imagine these people living flawless lives. But the truth is, we only see a sliver of their reality—the polished parts they choose to show. It's human nature to compare ourselves to others and use them as a measuring stick for our worth. And when we feel insecure or inadequate, those comparisons can become even more distorted.

When we compare ourselves, especially in areas where we feel vulnerable or lacking, we tend to focus on what others seem to excel at while we overlook their struggles. Our insecurities cloud our perception, and make it easy to assume that 'they' have what we don't—success, beauty, confidence, or happiness. Social media only makes this worse, all it does is offer a carefully curated highlight reel that fuels the illusion of perfection. On top of that, cultural and societal pressures make us feel like we should constantly strive for an impossible ideal.

But here's the truth: perfection is just that—an illusion.

No one lives a life without flaws, setbacks, or insecurities. The people we think are perfect are just as human as we are. We only see the surface, not the whole story. Think about someone you've compared yourself to recently. What is it about them that seems 'perfect'? Now, consider that what you see is a fraction of their lives. Are you playing witness to the whole picture?

The Saved by the Bell Effect

Let's step back to one of the most iconic TV moments—the Saved by the Bell episode in which Jessie Spano's perfectionism spirals out of control.

Jessie is the ultimate high-achiever:
- Straight A's
- Student leadership
- Extracurriculars
- An unrelenting drive to be the best

But as her commitments pile up, so does the pressure. Instead of slowing down, she convinces herself she needs a 'little boost' to keep up.

Enter caffeine pills.

At first, it seems like the perfect fix—she's awake, energetic, and on top of everything. But as the pressure builds, so does her anxiety. When it's finally time to rehearse, she breaks down and utters the now-famous line: *"I'm so excited, I'm so excited... I'm so... scared."*

Jessie's meltdown wasn't just a dramatic TV moment but a reflection of the perfectionist paradox. The same drive that fuels success also fuels anxiety, burnout, and emotional collapse.

For many perfectionists, the coping mechanisms might not be caffeine pills, but they could be:
- Overwork to the point of exhaustion
- Procrastination because nothing ever feels 'good enough.'
- Avoidance of challenges out of fear of failure
- Seeking validation from others instead of self-acceptance

If this sounds familiar, you are not alone.

Activity: Reflect on Your Perfectionist Tendencies

Jessie's story might feel familiar to you. Maybe you also push yourself to the limit, constantly chasing perfection, only to feel exhausted and unfulfilled.

Take a moment to reflect on these questions:
1. **Where in your life do you feel the pressure to be perfect?**
   - Is it at work, in relationships, or in your appearance?
2. **How does perfectionism show up in your daily decisions?**
   - Do you put off tasks because they might not be good enough?
   - Do you often redo things over and over?
3. **What's the cost of your perfectionism?**
   - Has it affected your time, energy, or mental health?

Write down your answers. The goal isn't to 'fix' anything—it's just to notice. Once you become aware of these patterns, you can shift your approach.

Exercise: Self-Assessment Quiz on Perfectionism Traits

We've compiled a brief self-assessment on perfectionism traits to help you understand how perfectionism impacts your life. This is not a diagnostic tool but rather a way to understand the degree to which you may struggle with perfectionism.

Remember, this is not a competition to see who is most perfectionistic, nor is it meant to shame those with high perfectionistic tendencies. It's simply a tool to help you understand yourself better.

Instructions:
For each statement, choose the response that best describes how often you experience or feel this way:
- **Always (A): 3 points**
- **Often (O): 2 points**
- **Sometimes (S): 1 point**
- **Never (N): 0 points**

Questionnaire:
1. I often redo tasks because I'm unsatisfied with the first result.
2. I frequently worry about what others think of my work or performance.
3. I tend to set extremely high goals and feel disappointed if I do not meet them.
4. I struggle to delegate tasks to others because they won't meet my standards.
5. When I receive feedback, I focus on the negative rather than the positive aspects.
6. I often spend much longer on tasks than necessary because I want them to be perfect.
7. I avoid starting projects if I'm unsure I can do them perfectly.
8. My work must be 100% perfect to be valuable.
9. I believe that mistakes are a sign of failure.
10. It's hard to 'relax' or 'do nothing'.
11. I often compare myself to others.
12. When others seem to be 'doing better' or share success with me, I feel bad about myself, jealous, or even angry.
13. I often feel stressed or anxious about my need to be perfect.

Score Guide:
Add up your points based on your responses to each question:
- **Always (A): 3 points**
- **Often (O): 2 points**
- **Sometimes (S): 1 point**
- **Never (N): 0 points**

Interpret Your Results:

- **24-39 points:** High perfectionistic tendencies. You may often find that perfectionism impacts your overall well-being and daily life.
- **15-23 points:** Moderate perfectionistic tendencies. While not always overwhelming, perfectionist behaviors are noticeable and sometimes problematic.
- **5-14 points:** Mild perfectionistic tendencies. You have some perfectionist habits, but they don't dominate your behavior.
- **0-4 points:** Little to no perfectionistic tendencies.

Pause for Reflection:
Your score: _____
Do you agree or disagree with the results? Why or why not?

_____
_____
_____
_____

Remember, the idea behind the assessment is to set you on a path for self-reflection. Regardless of your score, if you feel that perfectionism harms your life, it may be worthwhile to explore this further, either through self-help resources or with the guidance of a mental health professional.

Activity: Perfectionism Inventory
Instructions:
Sometimes, the best way to understand your patterns is to slow down and look at them without judgment. This exercise is a gentle invitation to do just that.

Grab your journal, your favorite pen, maybe even a cup of tea. You're not here to fix anything but to listen to yourself.

Start by thinking back over the past week. Choose a few moments—maybe three, maybe five—where something inside you said: *"That wasn't enough."*

Now, write them down. For each one, ask yourself:
- What was happening around you?
- What were you trying to do?
- How did you feel when it didn't go how you hoped?
- What story did your mind start telling you?

Was it frustration? Shame? That old ache of *"I should've done better"*? Once the moments are on the page, take a breath. Then ask:
- If I hadn't been so hard on myself, how might I have responded instead?
- Could I have offered myself grace instead of guilt?
- What would it look like to *choose progress over perfection* in that moment?

Lastly, step back and look for patterns. Are your perfectionist tendencies tied to a particular area of life, like work, parenting, relationships, or how you show up for others?

And here's the big one:
What might shift if I loosened perfection's grip? What would be possible if I let 'good enough' *be* enough?

This isn't about getting it right. It's about getting honest with kindness.

Chapter Summary

In this chapter, we peeled back the polished surface of perfectionism to uncover what truly drives it. It's not ambition—it's fear—a deep, quiet fear of not being enough. We looked at how striving for flawlessness often hides an ache for worthiness and how comparison, self-doubt, and pressure can quietly shape how we move through the world.

But we also offered a new lens—Adlerian psychology—that helps explain these patterns with compassion instead of criticism. Through stories, reflection, and exercises, we invited you to stop chasing perfection and start understanding the beliefs beneath it. Once you see the pattern clearly, you can begin to shift it.

Now that you've explored how perfectionism shows up in your life, the next step is to understand *where it came from*.

Perfectionism isn't random. It's deeply tied to how you've learned to view success, failure, and your sense of self.

In Chapter 2: The Unseen Blueprint of Your Life, we'll explore the early experiences, family roles, and cultural messages that helped shape your perfectionist mindset today.

When you understand where those beliefs came from, you can begin to rewrite them—and finally break free from the cycle of never feeling *"good enough."*

Perfectionism isn't a flaw—it's a strategy—a coping mechanism for managing the universal human feeling of inferiority. Understanding this helps us replace self-blame with compassion and strive for acceptance.

CHAPTER 2: THE UNSEEN BLUEPRINT OF YOUR LIFE

The way we see the world isn't inherited — it's invented.

Adler believed we each create a 'lifestyle' — a personal map for how to belong, matter, and stay safe.

Understanding The Subconscious 'Life Script' You Follow

We all walk through life carrying a kind of internal map. Most of us don't even know it's there. But this map quietly guides how we make decisions, see ourselves, and respond to challenges. The way we see the world isn't inherited — it's invented. Adler believed we each create a 'lifestyle'—a personal map for how to belong, matter, and stay safe. It's the story we've been telling ourselves for so long that it feels like the truth.

In Adlerian psychology, this internal map is called your 'lifestyle'—but not in the way we often use the word today. Here, 'lifestyle' doesn't refer to routines or habits, but rather your unique way of interpreting the world, formed from early experiences and beliefs. It's the subconscious script that guides your thoughts, relationships, and perfectionist tendencies. These beliefs shape your behavior, your relationships, and your view of self-worth.

If perfectionism has taken hold of your life, chances are your internal map has some old directions that no longer serve you. This chapter is about uncovering that blueprint—and deciding if it's still leading you where you want to go.

In this chapter, we will:
- Explore how childhood experiences shape our perfectionist tendencies.
- Identify the hidden beliefs and expectations that drive our actions.

- Introduce reflection exercises to help you recognize the patterns that guide your decisions.

Private Logic: The Quiet Voice Behind the Scenes

We all have a personal logic that explains the world to us—a set of beliefs stitched together from childhood experiences, family messages, and emotional memories. Adler called this *private logic*.

It's not always rational. It doesn't need to be. It just must feel true enough to guide your choices.

For perfectionists, private logic often whispers things like:
- *"Good enough is never enough."*
- *"If I slip up, I'll lose love or respect."*
- *"I have to prove I'm worthy, over and over."*

These beliefs often run in the background, like a silent operating system. They're not bad or shameful—they were survival tools. But when they go unchecked, they keep you stuck in cycles of self-doubt, overcompensation, and burnout.

Case Study: Sarah and the Fear of Imperfection

Meet Sarah. She's a talented writer with a sharp mind and a strong work ethic. But deadlines terrify her. Not because she's lazy, but because she's scared to start. Her private logic tells her: *"If it isn't perfect, it's not worth doing."*

So she overprepares. Rereads. Rethinks. Stares at a blinking cursor. And misses her deadline—not because she didn't care, but because her fear of imperfection shuts her down.

Sarah's not alone. This kind of internal script is common for perfectionists. It doesn't matter how much praise she gets—if her private logic says *"you're only as good as your last flawless result,"* anything short of that feels like failure.

Exercise: Explore Your Private Logic

Take a few minutes to reflect on your private logic. What unrealistic expectations or self-criticisms do you hold? Ask yourself:
- What's a belief I hold about making mistakes?
- Where did I learn that?
- Would I say the same thing to someone I love?

Now, try flipping that belief. For example:
"If I fail, I'll be rejected" becomes
"Even when I stumble, I am still worthy of love."

It might not feel natural at first. But this is how we begin to update the map.

Reflect Boldly: What's your inner script saying?

Pause for a moment. When you hesitate, procrastinate, or overprepare, what story is your mind telling you?

Try finishing this sentence:
"If I don't _____, then _____."

Bringing these thoughts into the open is the first step to challenging them.

Exercise: Adlerian Thought Record

Over the next week, keep a daily Adlerian Thought Record to capture moments when you experience perfectionist thoughts. For each thought, reflect on the following:

1. **Identify the thought:** What was the perfectionist's thought or belief?
2. **Trigger and context:** What triggered this thought? Was it a desire for superiority or a fear of inferiority?
3. **Feelings and behaviors:** How did this thought make you feel? What actions did it prompt?

4. **Lifestyle and private logic:** How does this thought fit into your life's map or private logic? Consider:
   - Does this thought stem from a childhood belief or goal?
   - Is it striving for an unattainable ideal (superiority) to compensate for feelings of inadequacy?
5. **Reframing with social interest:** Reframe the thought to encourage self-compassion and connection.

For example:
- Change: "*I must get this right, or I've failed.*" to
- "*I am valuable regardless of my achievements, and by sharing my imperfections, I connect more deeply with others.*"

How Childhood Shapes Our Hidden Map
We absorb messages from our family, teachers, peers, and society from a young age. These messages become the foundation of our core beliefs—what we think about ourselves, success, failure, and perfection.

'Thou Shalt Overcome.'
As we examine how early experiences shape our core beliefs, we must explore the mistaken attitudes we develop. As Adler suggests, these attitudes can either propel us toward growth or become barriers that hold us back.

From Anatomy of Jealousy pg. 17
"Discover the goal and the guiding or fictive image around which the whole lifestyle of the individual is developed or organized his design for living which grows out of his goal; and to determine the individuals' mistaken attitudes which are also inherent in his goal and the misconceptions about reality which are the basis of his discomfort or unhappiness."

It's vital to first understand your lifestyle and 'mistaken attitudes.' In Adlerian psychology, mistaken attitudes are negative thought patterns and beliefs that hinder personal growth and well-being. These beliefs, often formed early in life, can include exaggerated self-importance, an inferiority complex, self-centeredness, dependence, and avoidance of life's challenges. They can lead to problems in relationships, work, and overall life satisfaction. For example, someone might have mistakenly believed they must be perfect to be loved.

This can lead to constant self-criticism or overcompensation through achievements, which often strain relationships and create a cycle of stress and dissatisfaction.

A few ways to understand these mistaken attitudes include self-reflection practices like mindful meditation, body scans, and an intentional pause before you react when you feel emotional. For instance, the next time you feel a surge of anger or frustration, take a moment to pause. Instead of an immediate response, tune in to what's happening in your body and mind. Are you tense? Is it a belief that drives your emotional reaction, like *"I need to be in control"* or *"Things must go my way"*? This pause creates space for reflection, allowing you to consider how underlying beliefs or biases may influence your reactions.

Practice: Notice Without Judgment
Try this the next time you feel that internal pressure rise:
- Pause.
- Ask: *"What am I believing right now?"*
- Tune in to your body. Tight jaw? Racing thoughts?
- Name it. Gently.

Maybe it's: *"I'm scared this won't be good enough,"* or: *"I'm worried they'll think less of me."*

Don't try to fix it. Just notice it. That's where the shift begins.

Ask yourself, *"Is it true that I must be perfect to be of value? Could this feedback be an opportunity for growth rather than a reflection of my worth?"*

The key is not to label your thoughts or feelings as 'bad' or 'good.' When certain emotions or reactions come up, resist the urge to judge or fix them. Instead, aim to acknowledge and explore what they might be trying to tell you. This isn't about self-shaming or criticizing—it's about noticing with curiosity, not condemnation. Let's say you feel jealous of a friend's success. The goal isn't to scold yourself with thoughts like, *"I shouldn't be jealous—what's wrong with me?"* Instead, try simply naming the emotion: *"I feel jealous right now."* Then ask, *Why? What might this emotion be revealing?* Maybe it points to a fear of being left behind or a desire for more recognition in your own life. The insight lies in observing, not attacking.

This process is about **understanding** your emotions, not sorting them into 'good' or 'bad.' Feelings serve as signals, guiding you toward deeper beliefs or unmet needs. When you allow yourself to recognize them without being ruled by them, you gain clarity. It's like listening to your internal GPS. Sometimes, it reveals outdated beliefs or hidden fears you didn't even know were driving your behavior.

For example, if you often feel anxious when meeting new people, don't rush to silence that anxiety. Instead, ask yourself: *What belief is behind this?* You might realize you've been carrying the idea that *"People only like me if I'm perfect."* That belief likely traces back to a time when love or acceptance felt conditional. Seeing that clearly can be powerful.

You don't have to force the anxiety to go away. Just decide how you want to respond. Maybe you remind yourself, *"I don't have to be perfect to be liked. Everyone has insecurities—including me."* What matters isn't eliminating the feeling but choosing how to move through it. By practicing this kind of self-awareness and compassion, you start making decisions that support your well-being, instead of reacting on autopilot. That's where growth begins.

Now that we have explored how mistaken attitudes shape our perception of ourselves and our interactions with the world, the next step is to develop practical ways to shift those ingrained thought patterns.

Mistaken attitudes thrive in self-judgment and rigid thought cycles, but mindfulness offers a way out. To become more present and aware of our thoughts without immediately reacting to them, we create space to challenge limiting beliefs and instill a more compassionate self-narrative. Instead of getting caught up in the pressure to 'fix' ourselves or silence our insecurities, mindfulness encourages us to observe without judgment, accept without resistance, and redirect without force. Through the following mindfulness exercises, we will explore concrete strategies for practicing self-compassion, emotional regulation, and perspective-taking—key skills needed to break free from perfectionism's grip.

Recognizing our mistaken attitudes is only the first step. To truly reshape our relationship with perfectionism, we must practice being 'present with our thoughts and feelings' without judgment. This is where mindfulness and self-compassion come in, helping us gently shift from harsh self-criticism to self-acceptance.

Mindfulness Exercises to Overcome Mistaken Attitudes

These mindfulness exercises align with the previous section's discussion on recognizing mistaken attitudes and serve as practical applications of our self-reflection work so far. They will help you shift from over-identifying with perfectionistic beliefs to creating new patterns of self-acceptance and balance.

Exercise: Identify Energy 'Takers' and 'Givers'

Perfectionism often pushes us toward activities that drain us, leaving little room for restoration. By recognizing which activities deplete us and which ones replenish us, we can start making intentional choices that prioritize our emotional well-being.

1. Draw two columns on a piece of paper: One labeled *Energy Taking* and the other labeled *Energy Giving*.
2. In the *Energy Taking* column, list activities that drain you or leave you feeling exhausted. Some examples:
   - Overworking and saying yes to everything
   - Comparing yourself to others
   - Striving for perfection instead of progress
3. In the *Energy Giving* column, list activities that nourish you. Some examples:
   - Going for a walk in nature
   - Spending time with a friend who uplifts you
   - Reading a book for pleasure

Reflection: Once you have completed both lists, reflect on their balance. Do you engage more frequently in energy-taking than energy-giving activities? What minor adjustments can you make to introduce more balance?

Exercise: Box Breathing to Release Perfectionist Tension

When caught in mistaken attitudes, our nervous system often goes into overdrive, which leads to stress, frustration, and emotional exhaustion. Box breathing is a simple yet powerful technique that helps regulate the nervous system and creates space between reaction and response.

1. Find a comfortable seat and close your eyes.
2. Follow the 'box breathing' pattern:
   - Inhale for a count of 4
   - Hold for a count of 4
   - Exhale for a count of 4
   - Hold again for a count of 4
3. Repeat the cycle for at least five rounds, focusing on the rhythm of your breath.

Reflection: Once you complete the exercise, ask yourself: *"What sensations do I notice in my body? Do I feel more at ease? How might incorporating small moments of mindfulness like this shift my daily experience of perfectionism?"*

Exercise: Heart-Centered Meditation for Self-Compassion

Perfectionism often creates a harsh inner critic that keeps us locked in cycles of shame and self-doubt. This meditation practice allows us to reconnect with our compassionate selves, helping us rewrite internalized mistaken attitudes with kindness.

1. Close your eyes and place one hand on your heart.
2. Visualize a cozy, warm space behind your heart. Imagine this as your safe place—a space where all versions of yourself are welcome.
3. Invite in a younger version of yourself—the part of you that felt the pressure to be perfect. Picture them sitting in this warm space with you.
4. Now, invite someone who loves and supports you unconditionally. Imagine their warmth and kindness fill the space.
5. Spend a few moments here, soak in acceptance, compassion, and safety.

Reflection: What emotions surfaced during this meditation? How did it feel to offer compassion to yourself? How might you practice carrying this sense of self-acceptance into your daily life?

Exercise: 'Drop the Actor' – Release Your Perfectionist Roles

Many perfectionists unconsciously adopt roles or masks to present a flawless version of themselves to the world—whether it's the 'perfect employee,' the 'always-happy friend,' or the 'flawless parent.' This exercise invites you to step out of those roles and just be.

1. **Identify the roles you play.** Take a moment to recognize which roles exhaust you and feel inauthentic.
2. **Close your eyes and imagine physically taking off each role.** You are not throwing them away; you are just setting them aside for now.
3. **Sit with the feeling of just being.** No titles, no expectations—just you.

Reflection: How does stepping out of these roles feel, even for a moment? What does your authentic self feel like underneath the perfectionist armor?

Now that we've explored how mistaken attitudes shape our perceptions and emotions, let's apply mindfulness practices to develop a more compassionate relationship with ourselves. The following exercises will help you stay present, acknowledge your thoughts without self-judgment, and create healthier patterns of self-acceptance.

Mindfulness and Self-Compassion

This section will dive into mindfulness and self-compassion exercises to help you shift your focus from external comparisons and self-criticism to setting realistic and personal goals. Mindfulness isn't just about being present; it's about cultivating a kinder, more understanding relationship with yourself. By practicing mindfulness and self-compassion, you can create a space where you accept your feelings, thoughts, and imperfections without judgment. This helps reduce the grip of perfectionism and lays the foundation for a more compassionate way of striving toward your goals.

To practice mindfulness is not to eliminate thoughts or feelings, but to create space for them without giving them the power to define us. As we continue, we'll explore how self-compassion plays a key role in breaking free from perfectionism's grip.

Your Family Blueprint: Lessons You Didn't Know You Learned

Imagine a child who constantly hears, *"You need to be the best,"* or *"If you don't do well, you'll never succeed."* Over time, these words become a deeply ingrained belief that can lead to relentless self-criticism and a fear of falling short.

Alternatively, a child who grows up in an environment where failure is punished or ridiculed may develop anxiety about making mistakes. They may avoid risks, procrastinate, or constantly seek validation to prove their worth.

Here are some common perfectionist beliefs that develop early:
- *"I must be perfect to be loved."*
- *"Mistakes make me a failure."*
- *"If I don't succeed, I am not worthy."*
- *"I must always prove myself."*

Over time, these beliefs become invisible rules we follow without a reason to question them. They shape how we handle setbacks, how we view others, and how we define success.

Case Study: Elle and the Smart Girl Identity

Elle was always introduced as "our brilliant daughter." And she was proud of that—until she wasn't.

When she got a B in college, she cried in her car. She stayed silent instead of asking when she didn't have an answer in a meeting. Her identity had become so wrapped in being "the smart one" that any stumble felt like betrayal.

Elle's perfectionism wasn't about grades—it was about identity. Her map said: *"If I'm not impressive, I'm not lovable."*

Pause for Reflection: What Was Your Label?

Think back to your childhood. Did you have a 'title' in your family?
- The helper?
- The achiever?
- The strong one?
- The fixer?

What did that label teach you about your worth? And does that belief still fit the life you want today?

Write down any thoughts that come to mind—no judgment—just observation.

How Society Reinforces Your Hidden Map
While family plays a significant role, **society, culture, and media** also shape our hidden maps.

The Social Media Perfectionist Trap
We live in an era where social media reinforces perfectionism every day. The curated, polished versions of people's lives create an illusion that everyone else has it all together.

It's easy to fall into the trap of thinking:
- *"Everyone else is more successful."*
- *"No one else struggles like I do."*
- *"If I just work harder, I'll finally be happy."*

But here's the truth: You are comparing your behind-the-scenes reality to someone else's highlight reel.

Reality check: Even the most 'perfect' people you admire have struggles, insecurities, and imperfections. The difference? They don't always show them.

Activity: The Story, You Tell Yourself
To better understand your hidden map, try this simple but powerful exercise:

Step 1: Think of an area in your life where you feel pressure to be perfect (career, relationships, appearance, etc.).

Step 2: Complete this sentence:
   "I believe that if I _____, then I will finally _____."

Example:
- *"I believe that if I work harder, then I will finally feel worthy."*
- *"I believe that if I always make people happy, then I will finally be loved."*
- *"I believe that if I never make mistakes, then I will finally feel safe."*

Step 3: Ask yourself, **"Where did this belief come from?"** Was it something you were taught? Something you absorbed from culture? Something you saw modeled by others?

Step 4: Write it down. No judgment—just curiosity.

Rewriting Your Map: The Power of Awareness
The good news is this: your map is not permanent.

Adlerian Insight:
Adler believed that while our early experiences shape us, they don't define us. Once you see the rules you've been following, you can question them. Rewrite them. Choose a new route.

Maybe instead of:
   "If I'm not perfect, I'll be rejected."
You try:
   "I am human. Messy, growing, and still worthy."

That's not a weak compromise. That's healing.

Chapter Summary
In this chapter, we uncovered the hidden rules that have quietly shaped your perfectionism. From early childhood messages to the family roles you absorbed, we explored how your internal blueprint—your private logic—has guided how you see yourself and the world.

You've seen how mistaken attitudes can keep you stuck, even when they once kept you safe. And you've started learning how to pause, reflect, and gently challenge the old beliefs that no longer serve you.

The goal isn't to erase your past. It's to understand it, so you can choose something new.

Through reflection exercises and case studies, we examined:
- How family, teachers, and peers influence self-worth and perfectionist tendencies.
- How private logic and mistaken attitudes reinforce negative self-beliefs.
- How to challenge and reframe these perfectionist thoughts to create a healthier mindset.

Understanding the origin of perfectionism is the first step toward shifting our approach to success, failure, and self-acceptance. By recognizing the invisible map we've been following, we gain the power to redraw it to serve us better.

Now that we've uncovered the hidden map that shapes your thinking, the next step is to understand the inner battle that perfectionism creates—the constant tug-of-war between high expectations and self-doubt.

In Chapter 3: The Battle Between Who You Are and Who You Should Be, we'll explore:
- The inner dialogue of a perfectionist—how competing thoughts create mental tension.
- How cognitive dissonance fuels anxiety, procrastination, and self-sabotage.
- Practical strategies to navigate this internal struggle and find balance.

As you move forward, consider this: Do you ever feel like two parts of yourself are fighting for control—one pushes you toward perfection, the other warns you that it's never enough?

This next chapter will help you understand and untangle the internal conflict, giving you the tools to align your self-worth with a more sustainable, fulfilling path.

CHAPTER 3: THE BATTLE BETWEEN WHO YOU ARE AND WHO YOU SHOULD BE

When our sense of worth is tied to who we think we should be, we lose touch with who we truly are.

Adlerian theory views identity not as fixed, but as a creative, evolving response to early experiences and perceived expectations.

The Unrelenting Struggle Between Two Voices
Perfectionism is not just a set of high standards—it is an internal battle, a constant tug-of-war between two opposing forces.
- One side says, *"You need to work harder. You're not doing enough."*
- The other whispers, *"You're exhausted. Can't you ever take a break?"*

This tug-of-war creates an exhausting paradox: the more we achieve, the more we feel we need to prove ourselves. We live under constant pressure, striving to be our best, yet never allowing ourselves to feel we are enough.

Perfectionists experience this battle in every aspect of life. Whether they overwork, procrastinate, or feel like an impostor in their own success, the tension between striving for excellence and fearing inadequacy is relentless.

When our sense of worth is tied to who we think we should be, we begin to lose touch with who we truly are. Adlerian theory reminds us that identity is not fixed—it's a creative, evolving response to early experiences and perceived expectations.

In Adlerian psychology, the pursuit of superiority—our drive to improve, grow, and succeed—is a natural and healthy instinct.

The 'should-self'—that idealized version of who we think we must become—is often a distorted form of this superiority striving, shaped by early beliefs about what earns us love, acceptance, or safety. But when this striving is rooted in a fear of inadequacy, it can become a source of anxiety rather than motivation.

- **Striving for growth** → Leads to self-improvement and learning.
- **Striving to avoid failure** → Leads to self-criticism and burnout.

The perfectionist mind believes success is the only acceptable outcome. But here's the catch—perfection is an illusion. It keeps us in a cycle of proving, overworking, and fearing failure without ever allowing ourselves to feel accomplished.

Many perfectionists struggle with identity, not because they lack direction, but because their self-image is shaped more by internalized 'shoulds' than by their own desires or values. They spend so long becoming the person others admire that they lose track of who they really are.

Perfectionism doesn't appear in just one area of life—it spreads into everything we do. From career success to relationships and even hobbies, perfectionists often impose impossible standards on themselves. However, the problem with these high expectations is that they often lead to disappointment, frustration, and burnout. Let's take a closer look at how perfectionism tricks us into chasing the impossible.

Perfectionism's Trap: Why We Chase the Impossible
Perfectionists often impose idealized standards on themselves, believing they will finally feel good enough if they reach a specific goal.

But the problem is that perfection is an illusion.

For example, imagine someone who starts a fitness journey with the belief: *"If I train daily, eat clean, and push myself, I'll look like a fitness model in three months."*

At first, they feel motivated. But when progress is slower than expected, frustration sets in. Instead of celebrating small wins, they fixate on how far they must go. This leads to self-doubt, exhaustion, and possibly giving up entirely.

Perfectionism shows up in many areas:
- **Career:** *"If I don't get this promotion, I'm not successful."*
- **Relationships:** *"I need to be the perfect partner, or I'll never be loved."*
- **Appearance:** *"If I don't look flawless, I'll be judged."*
- **Creativity:** *"If I can't create something perfect, why bother?"*

Perfectionists often impose idealized standards on themselves, demanding exceptionally high achievement and success. While focusing on desired outcomes and goals may seem healthy, problems arise when individuals cannot meet these high expectations.

If you are stuck in this perfectionist push-and-pull, this next exercise will help you shift from self-judgment to self-acceptance. It's time to challenge the idea that imperfection is a failure.

Adler taught us about the courage to be imperfect, highlighting how perfectionism often traps us in fear—the fear of making mistakes, the fear of judgment, and the fear of disappointing others. Embodying our imperfections means we allow true growth and happiness to emerge.

It's about shifting our focus from striving to be 'perfect' to being 'real' and 'authentic.'

Exercise: Acknowledge and Embrace Imperfections
Purpose:
List some imperfections you've been hesitant to share with the world. Next to each, write down something positive that could come from revealing this part of yourself. Perhaps your honesty, vulnerability, and openness to share about your struggles could help others feel less alone.

Reflect on how moving away from perfectionism and embracing imperfection can change your life. Consider the freedom it could bring, the energy you'd save, and how it might deepen your connections with others.

Case Study: Overcommitment and Burnout – Lindsay's Story
Meet Lindsay.

Lindsay used to believe that being busy meant she was doing something right. She felt like she was falling behind if she wasn't juggling a hundred different tasks.

She had convinced herself that if she just kept going, she'd finally feel satisfied. But in reality, she never did. No matter how much she accomplished, her mind would immediately move the goalpost:

- Finished a project? → *Great, but what's next?*
- Earned recognition? → *Enjoy it for a moment, then get back to work.*
- Took a break? → *Feeling guilty because she 'should' be doing more.*

Even though she was successful on paper, she was chronically exhausted, anxious, and afraid of slowing down.

The fear wasn't about failing—it was about feeling like she never did enough.

This is the tug-of-war of perfectionism: A constant cycle of overcommitment and burnout with no finish line in sight.

Pause for Reflection: The Cost of the Constant Push
Take a breath and ask yourself:
- Do I feel guilty when I rest?
- Do I move the goalpost as soon as I reach it?
- Does success bring relief—or more pressure?

Write down what comes up. You don't need to fix anything yet. Just notice.

If you find yourself stuck in this perfectionist push-and-pull, this next exercise will help you shift from self-judgment to self-acceptance. It's time to challenge the idea that imperfection is a failure.

The Inner Critic: Your Loudest Opponent
At the heart of this tug-of-war is the inner critic—a relentless voice that tells you:
- *"You're not trying hard enough."*
- *"You should be further ahead by now."*
- *"Other people don't struggle like this."*

Perfectionists often internalize harsh self-judgment, making it difficult to feel proud of their accomplishments. Even success feels fragile, as though it could be taken away at any moment.

Adlerian Insight:
The inner critic is not an objective truth-teller. It is a learned voice, often rooted in childhood messages about success, self-worth, and achievement.

Over time, these critical thoughts become automatic. They dictate how we measure our worth and convince us that we are only as valuable as our last achievement.

Pause for reflection: Recognize Your Inner Struggle.
Take a moment to reflect on how perfectionism shows up in your daily life:
- Do you constantly feel like you need to prove yourself?
- Does success bring relief, or just pressure to do more?
- Are you more critical of yourself than you would be of a friend?

Write down any thoughts that arise—awareness is the first step toward breaking free.

Activity: Rewrite Your Inner Dialogue
Objective:
This exercise helps shift harsh self-criticism into self-compassion, allowing you to reframe your inner dialogue.

Instructions:
1. **Write down a common phrase your inner critic says.**
   - Example: *"I never do anything right."*
2. **Imagine saying this to a close friend.**
   - Would you speak to them this way? What would you say instead?
3. **Reframe it with self-compassion.**
   - Example: *"I make mistakes, just like everyone else. I am learning, and that's okay."*
4. **Read the new phrase out loud.** Notice how it feels to speak to yourself with kindness.

Reflection Prompt:
How does it feel to shift from self-judgment to self-acceptance? What would change in your life if you consistently practiced this?

Activity: Identify Your Perfectionist Rules
One reason perfectionism is so challenging to overcome is that we create rigid, unrealistic rules for ourselves.

Try this exercise:
Step 1: Write down one perfectionist rule you live by.

Example: *"I must always be productive."*

Step 2: Ask yourself, *"Where did this rule come from? Was it taught to you? Did you pick it up from culture or family?"*

Step 3: Challenge it—is this rule fair? Would you impose it on someone you love?

Example:
Perfectionist Rule: *"If I don't get everything right, I fail."*
New Perspective: *"Mistakes are proof that I am learning."*

Break Free: The Role of Self-Compassion
The only way to escape the perfectionist tug-of-war is to stop seeing self-worth as something you must constantly earn.
- Self-compassion is not 'giving up.'
- It's treating yourself with the same kindness you show others.
- It's to recognize that you are worthy, even when you are not perfect.

Adlerian Insight:
We don't have to be perfect to be valuable. Our worth is not based on achievements but on our ability to learn, grow, and connect with others.

Chapter Summary
In this chapter, we explored the inner battle between your authentic self and the version of you that perfectionism demands.

We looked at how perfectionism promises success but delivers burnout, how it fuels an inner critic that measures your worth by your productivity, and how that pressure disconnects you from who you are.

You've learned that you don't have to choose between ambition and rest, growth and grace. The goal isn't to stop striving—it's to stop *suffering*.

When you lead from your true self, not your should-self, you create from love, not fear. And that changes everything.

The key takeaway? Perfectionism is not about working harder—it's about learning to let go of impossible standards and treat yourself with kindness.

Now that we've explored the internal battle of perfectionism, the next step is understanding where these beliefs began.

In Chapter 4: The Perfectionist Child and the Roles We Play, we'll explore:
- How birth order and family roles influence perfectionist tendencies.
- Why do some children become overachievers while others fear failure?

- Exercises to help you break free from childhood patterns of perfectionism.

As you move forward, reflect on this:
Did your family dynamics shape how you handle success, failure, and expectations today?

You don't need to destroy your 'should' self—you only need to meet it with compassion and curiosity. When you do, you'll find space to grow not from fear, but from kindness.

Chapter 4 will uncover the roots of these perfectionist beliefs and give you the tools to reshape them for a healthier future where you can live well despite perfectionism.

PART II: WHERE PERFECTIONISM BEGINS

Perfectionism doesn't arise in isolation—it has roots in childhood experiences, family roles, and cultural expectations. Adlerian psychology emphasizes that we interpret our experiences uniquely, forming private logic that governs our beliefs. If you grew up equating love with achievement or acceptance with flawlessness, you likely carried these beliefs into adulthood.

In Part II, we uncover how your past shaped your perfectionism—not to place blame, but to gain awareness and start making new choices.

Chapter 4: The Perfectionist Child and the Roles We Play— How birth order and family expectations shape self-worth.

Chapter 5: Childhood Lessons That Shaped Your Standards— Understand how childhood experiences create lifelong patterns.

Chapter 6: Chase the Impossible Dream — How perfectionism becomes a life-long pursuit for validation.

CHAPTER 4: THE PERFECTIONIST CHILD AND THE ROLES WE PLAY

The harsh voice inside isn't your enemy — it's a coping strategy turned against you.

Adler saw self-doubt not as failure, but as a signal that the striving for superiority has lost its way.

Family Constellation and Its Relationship to Perfectionism

Understanding one's family constellation is a cornerstone of Adlerian psychology. This chapter delves into the intricate dynamics of the family structure, exploring how these relationships profoundly shape our psychological makeup. From the roles we adopt within our families to the impact of our birth order, each element molds our perceptions, behaviors, and life choices.

Adler believed that examining these early social influences can uncover the root causes of our current challenges and motivations. In this part, we'll guide you through analyzing your family roles, understanding the implications of your birth order, and interpreting your early memories. Through reflective exercises and insightful examples, you will better understand how your earliest social interactions and family dynamics have crafted the person you are today.

The Family as the First Blueprint

You were part of a system long before you stepped into the world alone. Your family was your first blueprint for how the world works. Whether spoken aloud or silently felt, messages were sent:

- *"You're the responsible one."*
- *"You always get it right."*
- *"We don't show weakness here."*
- *"Be the best—or don't bother at all."*

Maybe love was tied to achievement. Maybe comfort came only when you performed.

Maybe being 'low maintenance' was the only way to avoid conflict. These patterns were never meant to hurt you—they were survival strategies. But they still shaped how you see yourself now.

Adlerian Insight:
According to Adlerian psychology, family dynamics are crucial in forming personality and self-concept. Birth order, parental expectations, and childhood roles influence our belief systems, especially for perfectionists.

In this chapter, we will explore:
- Birth order and how it influences perfectionism.
- Common family roles that contribute to perfectionist thinking.
- The hidden messages children receive about success, failure, and self-worth.

By understanding our family blueprint, we can begin to challenge the beliefs we inherited and reshape our relationship with perfectionism.

The Roles We Inherit

The harsh voice inside isn't your enemy; it's an old coping strategy that once protected you but now holds you back. Adler didn't see self-doubt as a flaw but as a signpost, evidence that one's striving for superiority has veered off course and needs redirection, not shame.

Our perfectionist tendencies don't just appear out of nowhere, they're often shaped by the environments we grew up in, especially our family dynamics. Whether it's pressure to meet high expectations, a need to please others, or even the desire to avoid conflict, these patterns can run deep and affect how we show up in the world.

In most families, children naturally fall into specific roles. These aren't chosen, but absorbed. They form quietly, sometimes out of necessity, to fill a gap.

Some common roles?
- **The Overachiever:** Praised for being the best, terrified to fall short.

- **The Peacemaker:** Keeps the peace at any cost, often silencing their needs.
- **The Caretaker:** Takes emotional responsibility for others, even as a child.
- **The 'Easy' One:** Avoids trouble, stays invisible, flies under the radar.
- **The Performer:** Earns love through charm, achievement, or perfection.

If you're a perfectionist, chances are your role was built around being exceptional, pleasing, or emotionally self-sufficient. That role became part of your adaptive self—your way of fitting in, staying safe, and feeling seen. But adaptation isn't always authenticity. With time, what once protected us may begin to limit us.

Birth Order and Perfectionism

In Adlerian theory, birth order is not a rigid label but a lens through which we can understand how children adapt to find belonging within their family system. These tendencies are responses, not definitions. The order in which we are born into our family, whether as an only child, the oldest, the middle, or the youngest, plays a crucial role in shaping how we view the world and interact with others.

Your position in the family often influences how perfectionism takes hold:

- **Firstborns** often carry the weight of responsibility. They may feel pressure to perform, model success, and avoid failure. Praise came early—but so did high expectations.
- **Middle children** sometimes feel overlooked. They may strive to stand out by being exceptional, adaptable, or agreeable. Perfectionism becomes a way to be noticed.
- **Youngest children** are often expected to entertain, excel, or stay easy-going. They might internalize a need always to be "fun" or never cause problems, masking more profound anxiety with overperformance.
- **Only children** may grow up with adult expectations from a young age. They often learn to be mature, conscientious, and self-sufficient, but may also struggle with internal pressure to always be 'on.'

These are tendencies, not templates. But when childhood roles go unexamined, they often follow us into adulthood. The 'responsible one' may grow into a proving adult. The 'peacemaker' might become someone who silences their needs. What once earned belonging may now be draining your sense of self. But understanding the patterns gives you language for your lived experience—and the power to rewrite it.

Caroline's Story: The Oldest Daughter

As the oldest daughter, Caroline quickly learned that her worth was tied to being dependable. She helped care for her siblings, excelled in school, and made sure not to cause waves. When she succeeded, she was praised. When she faltered, she felt invisible.

As an adult, she found herself trying to be everything for everyone: the high achiever, the helper, the one who always had it together. But beneath that competence was exhaustion. Her perfectionism wasn't ambition—it was a long-standing belief that her value came from being useful and flawless.

Activity: What Role Did You Play?

Take a moment to reflect. Growing up...
- What were you praised for?
- What was expected of you—spoken or unspoken?
- Were mistakes met with grace or disappointment?
- What role did you fall into to keep the peace, earn love, or feel safe?

Write freely. Don't edit—just notice.
Then ask: Does this role still define me today? Do I want it to?

While birth order provides one lens through which to view perfectionist tendencies, our specific family roles often deepen these patterns. Each family member unconsciously adopts a role based on early experiences, shaping their beliefs, behaviors, and coping mechanisms. Understanding these roles provides deeper insight into how we approach success, failure, and self-worth.

One of Adler's most influential ideas was that birth order plays a fundamental role in shaping personality.

Pause for Reflection:
Reflect on how your family environment reinforced or challenged these patterns. Birth order alone does not define us—it is intertwined with the unique roles and expectations placed upon us within our family constellation.

Reflection Questions:
- How has your birth order shaped your relationships with your family and others?
- Are there any specific examples from your life that illustrate the typical traits of your birth order?
- What expectations did your family have for you based on your position? How did these expectations shape your sense of self-worth?
- Beyond birth order, what other roles did you adopt in your family? Were you the peacemaker, the achiever, the caregiver? How did these roles reinforce or challenge your birth order traits?
- Did your family dynamics change over time (due to divorce, remarriage, loss, or other shifts)? If so, how did this affect your role in the family?

Now that you have a clearer picture of the influence of your birth order, let's take this further. Your role in the family is not just shaped by when you were born—it's also about the entire family constellation. Who surrounded you? What dynamics influenced you? Let's explore how these relationships worked together to shape your perfectionist tendencies.

The Family as a Mirror: How Parents Model Perfectionism
Children absorb their parents' values, expectations, and anxieties—often without realizing it.

Children internalize those messages if a parent is highly self-critical, overworked, or driven by achievement.
- Did your parents set extremely high standards?
- Were mistakes met with criticism or patience?
- Did you feel loved for who you were, or only when you achieved?

Pause for Reflection:
1. What messages did you receive about success and failure as a child?
2. Were mistakes in your home treated as learning experiences or something to avoid?
3. How do these early messages still influence how you view yourself today?

Adlerian Insight:
Children unconsciously imitate their caregivers. If perfectionism is modeled as the standard, they carry it into adulthood unless they learn to challenge it.

Case Study: Lisa's Story
Meet Lisa.

Lisa grew up in a family where success was the unspoken currency of love. Her father, a successful business owner, had high expectations for all his children, while her mother managed the home meticulously, ensuring everything appeared flawless. While Lisa's siblings seemed unaffected by the pressure, Lisa internalized it. She believed that if she did not excel, she was failing. There was no middle ground.

Throughout school, Lisa worked tirelessly to achieve top grades, excel in sports, and be the 'perfect daughter.' Mistakes weren't an option, and any slip-up was a personal failure. As she grew older, this drive for perfection followed her into her career, relationships, and personal life. On the outside, Lisa seemed to have it all together—a successful job, a clean and organized home, always dressed nicely with her face and hair flawless—but internally, she was constantly overwhelmed, anxious, and always waiting for the moment when it all would fall apart.

It wasn't until later in life that Lisa began to unpack how her family's dynamics had shaped her perfectionism. She realized that her father's high expectations and her mother's obsession with outward appearances had created an invisible pressure never to show weakness and always be 'on.' Through therapy, personal growth, and acceptance, Lisa began to untangle her worth from her achievements, learning that her value didn't depend on perfection.

Family Roles and Their Psychological Impact
Adlerian theory suggests that our earliest memories provide key insights into our lifestyle, shaping how we interact with the world, perceive ourselves and others, and confront challenges.

These memories are not random—they carry emotional significance and contribute to the unconscious life script that guides our decisions and relationships.

Recall Early Memories
To fully understand your role in your family, start by recalling vivid early memories—especially those before age ten. Memories that arise spontaneously are often the most authentic, as others' retellings haven't influenced them.

Each memory is a narrative that reveals your early interactions with the world. Consider these points when you analyze your recollections:
- **Context:** Where and when did the memory occur? Who was present?
- **Emotions:** What feelings are associated with this memory?
- **Outcomes:** What was the result or conclusion of the events in the memory?

These recollections serve as windows into the unspoken rules of your childhood environment, highlighting how you learned to navigate approval, expectations, and self-worth.

Reflection Questions
As you reflect on your family role, ask yourself:
- Did you feel the need to meet high expectations in order to be accepted?
- Were you seen as the 'responsible one,' the 'peacemaker,' or the 'troublemaker'?
- How did your family dynamics reinforce these roles?
- Do you still find yourself living out aspects of this role today?

Remember that these roles are not binding.

Your answers may reveal subconscious patterns that still influence your perfectionism today. To take this insight further, let's map your family constellation in the next section.

Map Your Family Constellation

Start by creating a visual representation of your family constellation. This can be as simple as a family tree or a more detailed diagram highlighting key relationships, roles, and dynamics. Consider how each relationship has shaped your views on perfection. For example, was there a parent whose approval you were always seeking? A sibling you compared yourself to? As you map this out, consider how these roles may have influenced your need to be 'perfect.' The idea here isn't to assign blame but to notice the patterns that might still impact your life approach. When you see it on paper, it's easier to understand how family dynamics can create certain expectations and pressures, often leading to perfectionism. This step is about recognizing those influences and shifting away from them. Take your time with this.

It's not about getting it right but about noticing.

- What do you see in your family constellation?
- How might those dynamics have contributed to your perfectionism?

After mapping your family constellation, you may start to recognize patterns that have influenced your identity and behavior. Beyond birth order and relationships, families also pass down unconscious 'scripts'—unspoken rules and expectations that dictate how we view success, responsibility, and personal identity. These scripts can be empowering and limiting, shaping our self-worth and perfectionist tendencies in ways we may not even realize.

Now that we've explored how early family roles shape perfectionism, reflect on your experiences. The following exercise will guide you in rewriting roles that no longer serve you.

Exercise: Your Role in Your Family and Your Perfectionist Tendencies

Objective: Relate family constellation concepts to personal experiences of perfectionism.

Exercise:
- Draw a diagram of family structure, noting expectations, attitudes toward success and failure, and impactful interactions.
- Reflect on how relationships and expectations shaped perfectionist behaviors.

Reflection Questions:
- Which family dynamics contribute most significantly to perfectionistic traits?
- How might understanding these influences help address and alter perfectionist tendencies?

Additional Tips:
- **Role Play:** Explore family scenarios with a therapist or group to uncover unrecognized impacts of dynamics.
- **Therapeutic Dialogue:** Discuss family dynamics in therapy to uncover deeper emotional patterns.
- **Continued Learning:** Read more about Adlerian psychology's perspective on family constellations for a deeper understanding.

Activity: Rewrite Your Role in Your Family

To help break free from early family expectations, try this exercise:

Step 1: Identify the role you played in your family (**Example:** *"The Responsible One"* or *"The One Who Never Failed"*).

Step 2: Write down the hidden message you absorbed (**Example:** *"I must always be strong"*).

Step 3: Reframe it with a new, healthier belief (**Example:** *"I am worthy, even when I struggle"*).

Rewriting old beliefs, roles, and narratives is essential to recovering from them. They are fragile in their infancy and should be protected, practiced, and repeated to ensure their lasting impact on the life you want to build outside the constraints of perfectionism.

The following section offers a perspective on family scripts; it allows you to explore how these invisible narratives influence your personality and actions.

Family Scripts: The Unwritten Rules That Shape Us

Family scripts are unconscious, generational narratives that shape how family members respond to life challenges, expectations, and decision-making. These scripts often dictate what is considered 'acceptable' within the family and can influence everything from career choices to how we handle failure.

According to Adlerian psychology, family scripts are deeply ingrained in our lifestyle and identity. They reinforce birth order roles and perfectionist tendencies by creating rigid standards for how we should behave. Many perfectionists internalize these scripts, believing they are somehow 'failing' or letting their family down if they stray from them.

Common Examples of Family Scripts

Some examples of generational scripts include:
- *"We never quit—no matter what."*
- *"Failure is not an option in this family."*
- *"We always put others before ourselves."*
- *"In our family, success means hard work and sacrifice."*
- *"Our family has a reputation to uphold."*

These phrases might seem harmless, but they can create psychological stress if they become rigid expectations rather than guiding values.

Activity: Tracing Your Perfectionist Beliefs to Family Messages
Objective:
This exercise will help uncover which family messages shaped your perfectionist tendencies and how they influence your self-worth today.

Instructions:
1. Write down a core perfectionist belief you hold.
   - **Example:** *"If I don't succeed, I am not worthy."*
2. Identify the family message that reinforced this belief.
   - **Example:** *"My parents always praised me when I won but ignored my efforts when I failed."*
3. Examine the impact.
   - How has this belief shaped your career, relationships, or self-esteem?

4. Challenge it with a new perspective.
      - **Example:** *"I am valuable because of who I am, not just what I achieve."*
   5. Write a new, self-affirming belief to replace the old one.
      - **Example:** *"Mistakes are a natural part of growth, not a sign of failure."*

Reflection Prompt:
What emotions arise when you examine these family messages? How might changing this belief affect your life moving forward?

Exercise: Identify and Challenge Family Scripts
Use the next steps to identify and analyze the impact of family scripts in your life:
   1. **Identify common scripts:** Think about messages you heard repeatedly while growing up. What phrases or unspoken expectations were emphasized? How have these scripts shaped your beliefs about achievement, self-worth, or failure?
   2. **Understand script origins:** Trace these scripts back—who in your family embodied them? Were they based on culture, personal experiences, or generational trauma?
   3. **Assess script impact:** Are these scripts helpful or harmful? Have they pushed you toward perfectionism or limited your ability to take risks and embrace imperfection?

Family scripts shape our unconscious expectations and roles, and may contribute to deep-seated wounds that manifest as family trauma. These unspoken rules and inherited narratives often carry emotional weight, which reinforces cycles of perfectionism, self-doubt, or fear of failure. When these patterns become ingrained, they can lead to trauma responses that affect our relationships, self-esteem, and overall well-being. An essential step to living well with perfectionist tendencies is to understand and address family trauma.

Healing from Family Trauma
Before we can begin healing, it's essential to recognize how trauma manifests in our daily lives. Understanding the symptoms and their impact allows us to take meaningful steps toward processing past experiences and reshaping our present.

Family trauma involves painful experiences within the family, such as loss, neglect, emotional or physical abuse, or high expectations that lead to deep-seated fears of failure. These experiences don't just stay in the past—they continue shaping how we view ourselves and interact with others.

Theoretical Background

According to Adlerian psychology, healing from family trauma requires more than just understanding the past—it's about recognizing how early patterns continue to affect your present. This means identifying the roles you played within your family and shifting the narratives that still hold power over you today.

Understanding Trauma and Its Symptoms

Trauma can manifest as anxiety, depression, difficulty in trusting others, and unstable relationships. Recognizing these signs is crucial for beginning the healing process.

Identify Family Trauma

Many perfectionists carry trauma-related beliefs that impact their self-esteem and coping strategies. Signs of unresolved family trauma might include:

- Chronic self-doubt or fear of rejection
- Struggles with emotional regulation or trust
- A persistent need to prove worth through achievements

When you consider your own experiences, what signs stand out for you?

Healing from family trauma is a deeply personal and ongoing process. It involves understanding the past, acknowledging its impact on the present, and taking active steps towards a healthier future. When you engage in these exercises and reflections, you can start to untangle the complex web of emotions and behaviors associated with your family history. This will pave the way for resilience and empowerment and enable you to break negative cycles that keep you from feeling at peace with your imperfections.

When to Seek Professional Support

As you begin reflecting on past experiences, especially those tied to family pain or trauma, it's important to recognize when support is needed. Some wounds run deep and deserve more than silent endurance.

If, as you read this chapter, you felt overwhelmed, frozen, or triggered by memories or emotions, that's not a sign of weakness. It's a signal from your body and nervous system that you're carrying something heavy, and you don't have to carry it alone.

Working with a licensed therapist or counselor can be a powerful step in your healing journey. Therapists trained in trauma-informed care or Adlerian therapy can help you process painful experiences in a safe, supported space. You'll be guided not just to unpack the past, but to reframe your story with compassion, clarity, and strength. Sometimes the most courageous thing you can do is ask for help. Healing doesn't have to happen in isolation, and often, it shouldn't.

If you're ready to go deeper, reach out. You're not broken—you're becoming.

Break The Cycle of Family Trauma:

- **Open Communication:** Encourage an environment where family members feel safe to express their thoughts and emotions without fear of judgment. This openness encourages trust and mutual understanding.
- **Shared Problem-Solving:** Work together to solve family challenges, which enhances teamwork and shared responsibility.
- **Celebrate Successes:** Make it a point to celebrate individual and family achievements. This practice boosts morale and reinforces the value of mutual support.
- **Resilience Reflection:** Reflect on a past situation where your family overcame a challenge. What strengths did each family member contribute? What lessons did you learn about your family's ability to cope and adapt?

- **Role-Play Scenarios:** Use role-play to practice responses to hypothetical stressful situations. This can help prepare family members for handling real-life challenges and improve their problem-solving skills.

Building family resilience is a dynamic process that requires time, effort, and commitment from all family members. It involves strengthening relationships, enhancing communication, and developing effective coping strategies. Families can survive and thrive in adversity by focusing on these areas, creating a legacy of strength and unity.

Analyzing Trauma's Impact
Reflect on how your trauma has shaped your perspective on relationships, self-worth, and life decisions. This insight can lessen trauma's influence over your life.

Exercise: Healing Trauma
Use the following exercises to address and process family trauma:
1. **Trauma Timeline:** Write down major life events that might contribute to your perfectionism. Reflect on how each shaped your behavior.
2. **Letter Writing:** Write a letter to a family member involved in your trauma. You don't have to send it—this is for you to express emotions freely.
3. **Safety Plan:** Identify healthy strategies to 'cope' and support systems to manage your emotional triggers.

Reflection Questions
- How has family trauma impacted your sense of trust and safety in relationships?
- What coping strategies have you found effective or ineffective in dealing with family trauma?
- How can you cultivate a supportive network that respects your healing journey?
- What is the most memorable observation from your family while growing up?

Healing from family trauma is an ongoing process; it's not about erasing the past but about reclaiming control over your present. These exercises can help you process emotions and develop resilience, allowing you to redefine your story to support self-acceptance rather than perfectionism.

Pause for Reflection:
1. How did it feel to challenge the role you played in your family?
2. What emotions came up when you rewrote your perfectionist script?
3. What is one small step you can take this week to embrace your new, healthier belief and heal from your family trauma?

Chapter Summary
In this chapter, we explored how perfectionism often starts in childhood, not as a personality flaw but as a response to the roles we were handed or the expectations we learned to carry. Maybe you were the 'responsible one,' the 'easy one,' the 'high achiever,' or the 'peacekeeper.' And maybe, without even realizing it, you built your identity around being good, helpful, or impressive.

These roles weren't wrong—they helped you navigate the world you were given. But over time, they can become rigid, exhausting, and hard to let go of, even when they no longer serve you.

By reflecting on your early family dynamics, birth order, and emotional responsibilities, you've begun to see how these patterns were formed. More importantly, you've started asking whether they align with who you are now, and who you want to become.

In Chapter 5 Childhood Lessons That Shaped Your Standards, we'll look at the invisible lessons you absorbed about worth, love, and achievement—and how those childhood beliefs continue to shape your standards today. This next chapter is about connecting the dots between the past and the pressure you may still feel to prove yourself now.

As you move forward, consider this:
Are there childhood memories—big or small—that still influence how you see yourself today? Chapter 5 will help you uncover and reshape those early experiences so they no longer control your perception of your self-worth.

CHAPTER 5: CHILDHOOD LESSONS THAT SHAPED YOUR STANDARDS

When approval becomes our compass, we lose sight of our own north.

Adlerian theory challenges us to shift from seeking praise to cultivating purpose and contribution.

The roots of praise-seeking often begin in childhood.

How Our Past Writes Our Story
Before we understood success, failure, or perfectionism, we had already absorbed messages about them.

As children, we interpreted every reaction, correction, or moment of praise through the lens of someone desperate to understand their worth.
- Did your teachers and parents reward achievement over effort?
- Were mistakes treated as lessons or as failures?
- Were you encouraged to take risks, or did you fear disappointing those around you?

By the time we reach adulthood, we rarely question the lessons we learned early on. These beliefs become the hidden rules we live by, often without realizing it.

Adlerian Insight:
Alfred Adler believed that childhood is when we develop core beliefs about ourselves. These early experiences shape what he called our 'private logic'—an internal set of rules that influences how we strive for success and interpret failure.

In this chapter, we will:
- Explore how childhood experiences planted the seeds of perfectionism.
- Examine the early beliefs we internalized about self-worth, achievement, and failure.
- Learn how to challenge and rewrite these childhood messages.

Let's continue to uncover the past so we can reshape our future.

Exercise: Make a Map of Your Perfectionist Patterns
Instructions:
Create a 'Perfectionism Map' by drawing a large circle on a piece of paper. Inside the circle, list different areas of your life (e.g., work, relationships, health, hobbies). Next, around each area, write down the specific perfectionist behaviors or thoughts you experience. Reflect on the following:
1. What patterns emerge in your pursuit of perfection in these areas?
2. How do these patterns shape your daily decisions?
3. What emotions accompany these perfectionist behaviors?

Purpose:
This exercise allows you to visualize how perfectionism invades various aspects of your life, developing your self-awareness of how your 'lifestyle' or personal map influences your behaviors and decisions.

The Hidden Messages of Childhood
Client Story: The First Time Perfectionism Took Root in E's Life

I remember the first time I felt like my worth depended on success. I was seven years old, standing before my class, nervously waiting for my teacher to grade my work. I worked tirelessly on my project, carefully tracing each letter and ensuring every answer was 'perfect.'

As the teacher handed it back, she smiled. *"Excellent work,"* she said. *"You are such a smart girl!"*

The rush of approval felt incredible, but at that moment, a belief was born:

- *If I do things perfectly, I will be loved and valued.*
- *Mistakes mean I am not good enough.*
- *I need to be perfect every time.*

That was the first seed, and like many perfectionists, I spent the next few decades watering it.

Our childhood environment is crucial in shaping how we respond to the world. From a young age, we develop unconscious strategies to help us navigate relationships, gain approval, and avoid feelings of inferiority. These coping mechanisms, known in Adlerian psychology as personality priorities, form the foundation for seeking validation and structuring our sense of worth.

For perfectionists, these priorities often become deeply ingrained, shaping how they respond to success, failure, and relationships. While Alfred Adler laid the foundation with his theory of lifestyle and the striving for significance, it was Israeli psychologist Dr. Nira Kfir who later expanded on this framework with her concept of personality priorities—Superiority, Control, Comfort, and Pleasing. These are unconscious strategies we develop early in life to manage feelings of inferiority and seek belonging or value.

Far from being flaws, these priorities are creative survival strategies—deeply embedded solutions we once relied on to feel safe, accepted, or significant. Over time, however, they can become rigid, making it difficult to respond flexibly to life's challenges.

As Adler described in Anatomy of Jealousy, our mistaken beliefs and goals often become the organizing force of our lifestyle, shaping not just how we act—but how we interpret and emotionally respond to the world around us. When perfectionism is present, these personality priorities can serve as invisible rules driving our behavior, rooted in a desire to compensate for the 'felt minus' and reach for the 'felt plus.'

The following exercise will help you evaluate how these patterns may be showing up in your life. By identifying your dominant priority and the perfectionist habits tied to it, you'll begin to see where your striving comes from—and what it's truly asking for.

Exercise: Perfectionism Inventory
Purpose:
Write down recent instances when you felt your efforts weren't enough and explore the emotions and thoughts associated with these moments.

Objective:
Identify instances where your perfectionistic tendencies emerge and evaluate their impact.

Activity:
1. List specific occasions from the past week when you felt your efforts were inadequate.
2. Describe the scenario, your reaction, and the outcome.

Reflection:
Analyze how these situations made you feel and consider alternative reactions.

Activity: Daily Perfectionism Diary
Objective:
Track your daily activities and pinpoint when perfectionist thoughts arise.

Activity:
Maintain a weekly daily diary, noting when a perfectionistic thought occurs and its trigger.

Reflection:
Review the diary to identify patterns and triggers of perfectionism and strategize ways to address them.

By engaging in these exercises, you can better understand the nature of your perfectionism and develop strategies to mitigate its harmful effects.

What's Your 'Personality Priority'?

Personality priorities are the unconscious strategies we develop early in life to navigate social dynamics and protect ourselves from feelings of inferiority. In Adlerian terms, these strategies help us move from the 'felt minus' (feeling inferior) to the 'felt plus' (feeling superior or worthwhile).

People typically adopt four main personality priorities:

1. Superiority, 2. Control, 3. Comfort, 4. Pleasing/Approval.
Each priority represents how individuals seek to feel important and valued and avoid negative feelings of worthlessness, insignificance, or failure.

Among the four personality priorities, superiority is most commonly linked to perfectionism. Perfectionists often equate their worth with their ability to achieve, perform, and excel.

Their private logic tells them that to be valued, they must be the best, whether in academics, career, or social status. This constant need to prove oneself fuels anxiety, self-doubt, and an unrelenting pursuit of flawlessness.

How Personality Priorities Develop

These personality priorities develop early in life, typically by age five. As children, we begin to form beliefs about what makes us valuable or significant based on the feedback we receive from our environment—parents, teachers, peers, and societal expectations.

In the example of superiority, a child may discover that they receive praise when they are 'the best,' by being the top student or the star athlete. Over time, they internalize the belief that their worth is tied to being the best. They feel inadequate when not recognized for their achievements (their 'felt minus'). To avoid this, they push themselves harder to reach the 'felt plus' of being superior, even though this cycle often leaves them drained.

Understanding your personality priority is an additional step toward breaking free from perfectionism. Once you identify how your priority drives your perfectionistic behavior, you can start making conscious changes to shift your mindset and behaviors.

- **Acknowledge the trade-off:** Recognize the price you're paying for maintaining your superiority complex (e.g., exhaustion, anxiety, overwork).
- **Challenge your beliefs:** Question the assumption that your worth is tied to being the best or achieving flawless outcomes.
- **Example:** As a workaholic, you might focus on doing your best and learning from your mistakes rather than feeling devastated when you can't achieve perfection.

Practice self-compassion: Allow yourself to be imperfect. Accepting that mistakes and flaws are part of being human reduces the pressure of always being perfect.

The Personality Priorities theory in Adlerian psychology offers valuable insights into why perfectionists are driven by an intense need to be the best or feel superior.

These personality priorities aren't signs of something wrong with you—they're creative responses to what you needed at the time. They helped you find connection, belonging, and a sense of self-worth in a world that may have felt uncertain or overwhelming. But now, as an adult, you have the opportunity to choose new ways of navigating life—ones rooted in compassion instead of fear.

By understanding these priorities, perfectionists can challenge the beliefs that fuel their need for perfection and develop healthier, more balanced ways of living.

Recognizing these patterns in your own life can help you make intentional changes, shifting your focus from needing to be perfect toward embracing your inherent worth regardless of your achievements.

Superiority as a Personality Priority

For perfectionists, superiority is often the dominant personality priority. People who prioritize superiority feel best about themselves when seen as being the best, most competent, or achieving the highest standards. They often believe their worth comes from being excellent, flawless, or outperforming others. This constantly pushes them to strive to be the best in everything they do.

- **Felt Plus:** When perfectionists are praised for their abilities, accomplishments, or intellect, they feel worthy. Achieving high grades, landing prestigious jobs, or being admired by peers temporarily satisfies them.
- **Felt Minus:** On the other hand, when perfectionists feel they are not living up to these high standards—whether through perceived failure, criticism, or lack of recognition—they experience intense feelings of worthlessness or insignificance.

This leads to shame, anxiety, or a fear of being 'found out' as inadequate.

Envision a student who has always been praised for their academic achievements. This praise reinforces their belief that their value comes from being the best student. If they ever receive a grade that isn't perfect, they might experience a sharp drop in self-esteem, believing they are no longer 'worthy.' To avoid these feelings of worthlessness, the individual might overwork themselves to maintain high grades, even at the expense of their well-being.

Adlerian Insight:

Adler believed that children are constantly making sense of their place in the world. If children only receive praise for achievements, they learn that their worth is conditional.

The School System and External Validation

For many perfectionists, school was the first place they learned that achievement = worthiness.

- Did you strive for gold stars, high grades, or the praise of teachers?
- Did you feel anxiety if you didn't meet expectations?
- Were you labeled as *"The smart one," "The responsible one,"* or *"The overachiever"*?

Letting Go of Superiority-Based Perfectionism

For those prioritizing superiority, perfectionism is deeply tied to their sense of worth. Their identity is built around being the best, achieving the highest standards, and proving competence. Letting go of this mindset requires a fundamental shift—from defining worth through external accomplishments to embracing inherent value, growth, and self-acceptance.

Control as a Personality Priority

For some perfectionists, control is the dominant personality priority. These individuals feel most secure when they can predict and manage their environment, decisions, and outcomes. Control-oriented perfectionists often believe that maintaining strict order and structure will prevent chaos, failure, or disappointment.

- **Felt Plus:** When they successfully organize every detail, anticipate potential problems, or enforce a sense of order, they feel a sense of security and competence. Having control over situations, projects, or relationships reinforces their belief that they are responsible and capable.
- **Felt Minus:** When things don't go as planned—when unexpected obstacles arise, others don't meet their high standards, or they feel powerless—they experience stress, frustration, or even panic.

This mindset often leads to hypervigilance and rigidity. Consider a person who meticulously plans every aspect of their work and personal life. They feel accomplished when everything is running smoothly, but if something deviates from their plan, like a last-minute change or a mistake, they experience intense anxiety or self-blame. They may exert even more control over future situations to avoid these feelings, creating a cycle that makes flexibility and adaptability difficult.

Break Free from Control-Based Perfectionism:

- Acknowledge that uncertainty is part of life and that perfection is an illusion.
- Recognize that trying to control everything often leads to more stress, not less.
- Practice allowing minor imperfections and unexpected changes to occur without reacting negatively.

Perfectionists prioritizing control may struggle with delegation, spontaneity, and trust. Learning to embrace uncertainty and imperfection can help them develop resilience and inner peace.

Comfort as a Personality Priority

For some, perfectionism is not about being the best or being in control; it's about avoiding discomfort, failure, or emotional distress. Those who prioritize comfort use perfectionism as a defense mechanism to minimize risk and maintain a sense of ease.

- **Felt Plus:** When they can stay in familiar, predictable environments and avoid criticism, they feel safe and at ease. They may avoid challenging tasks or high-pressure situations to prevent potential failure or stress.
- **Felt Minus:** When faced with discomfort, uncertainty, or the possibility of failing, they feel overwhelmed and anxious. Their fear of making mistakes or disappointing others leads them to procrastinate or avoid situations where they might not perform perfectly.

A person with a comfort-driven personality may avoid trying anything unfamiliar unless they feel confident they'll succeed. They might pass on applying for a promotion, stay quiet in meetings, or skip new hobbies altogether, because the risk of failure feels too big.

Rather than stretch themselves, they stick to what's familiar, even if it means missing out on growth.

Overcome Comfort-Based Perfectionism:
- Recognize that growth and learning require stepping into discomfort.
- Understand that mistakes are not failures but stepping stones to improvement.
- Challenge avoidance patterns by taking small, manageable risks.

Perfectionists who prioritize comfort must learn to tolerate discomfort and embrace failure as part of progress. By gradually exposing themselves to new challenges, they can develop greater confidence and resilience.

Pleasing/Approval as a Personality Priority

For those who focus on pleasing others and earning approval, perfectionism often ties directly to relationships. Their sense of worth feels linked to meeting expectations, making others happy, and avoiding criticism or disapproval.

- **Felt Plus:** They feel secure and valued when they receive praise, validation, or reassurance. Being dependable, accommodating, and admired gives them a sense of identity and connection.
- **Felt Minus:** When they sense disappointment, rejection, or criticism, they feel unworthy—or even ashamed. They may go to great lengths to maintain a polished, agreeable image to avoid conflict.

Someone who prioritizes approval might say yes to everything, even when it costs them rest, time, or peace. They often avoid setting boundaries or expressing their needs, worried that doing so will make them seem selfish or unlikable. Their perfectionism shows up in the constant effort to be everything to everyone—always kind, always helpful, always enough.

Let Go of Approval-Based Perfectionism:
- Recognize that others' opinions or approval do not determine your worth.
- Practice setting boundaries and saying no without guilt.
- Challenge the belief that being imperfect will lead to rejection or disapproval.

Perfectionists who prioritize pleasing others must learn to validate themselves rather than rely on external praise. By setting healthy boundaries and allowing themselves to be authentic, they can develop more profound self-acceptance and freedom from the pressure of approval.

Pause for Reflection: What Were You Taught About Success and Failure?
Before we move forward, let's pause and reflect on your childhood beliefs.
1. What did success look like in your childhood home?
   - Was it celebrated? Expected? The only option?
2. Were you praised for your effort or results?
   - Did you always feel pressure to achieve?
3. Based on your personality priority, how did these lessons influence the perfectionist tendencies you carried into adulthood?

Write down one childhood memory of success or failure that stands out.

Exercise: Identify Your 'Felt Plus' and 'Felt Minus' Moments
Objective:
To help you notice when perfectionism shows up in your life by identifying the moments when you feel 'less than' (your 'felt minus') and what you're aiming for when trying to be 'perfect' (your 'felt plus'). Understanding this can give you a clearer picture of how perfectionism bridges the gap between 'who you think you are' and 'who you think you should be.'

Instructions:
Think About a Recent Situation:
- Take a moment to think about a recent time when you felt pressure to be perfect. Maybe it was at work during a presentation, a family gathering, or even meal preparation.
- Write down what happened, and try to capture how you felt. For example, *"I felt anxious before presenting my ideas in the meeting."*

Identify Your 'Felt Minus':
- Now, ask yourself: What thoughts or feelings made you feel 'less than' in that situation? Did you feel like you weren't good, smart, or capable enough?
- Jot down those thoughts and feelings. For instance, *"I felt like I wasn't knowledgeable enough compared to my colleagues,"* or *"I was afraid they would think I wasn't prepared."*

Recognize Your 'Felt Plus':
- Next, think about what you were aiming for. What would 'perfect' have looked like in that situation? What were you trying to prove or achieve?
- Write down your 'felt plus.' For example, *"I wanted to be seen as the most competent person in the room,"* or *"I wanted everyone to think I had everything under control."*

Explore the Gap:
- Now, take a step back and look at the gap between your 'felt minus' and 'felt plus.' How was perfectionism trying to bridge this gap for you?
- Ask yourself: Did striving for your 'felt plus' help, or did it leave you feeling more stressed and disconnected? For example, *"I pushed myself to work late, but in the end, I was still worried I didn't do enough."*

Write Down Your Insights:
- Spend a few minutes writing down what you noticed. What patterns do you see? How does perfectionism play out in your day-to-day life? What's the cost of constantly trying to bridge this gap?
- Reflect on how these moments affect you. For example, *"I realized that my need to be seen as the best made me feel more isolated."*

Purpose:
This activity helps you build awareness around how perfectionism manifests in your life. When you identify your 'felt minus' moments—times you feel not enough—and your 'felt plus' moments—what you believe will finally make you feel worthy—you begin to notice something important: perfectionism often creates more stress and disconnection than the worth or acceptance you hoped to gain.

The goal isn't to fix these feelings immediately but to understand them. The more you see the pattern, the easier it becomes to loosen perfectionism's grip—and to move toward a more compassionate, balanced way of living and achieving.

Activity: Rewriting Childhood Messages About Perfectionism
Objective:
This activity will help you uncover the earliest perfectionist messages you received and actively rewrite them into healthier beliefs.

Instructions:
1. Recall a childhood moment when you learned that success = worth.
    - **Example:** *"My teacher only praised me when I got a perfect score, not when I tried my best."*
2. Write down the message you internalized from that moment.
    - **Example:** *"I am only valuable when I succeed."*
3. Examine how this belief impacts your life today.
    - How does it shape your work, relationships, or self-esteem?
4. Rewrite the message into a healthier belief.
    - **Example:** *"My worth is not based on achievement. I am valuable just as I am."*
5. Read the new belief out loud. Notice how it feels to shift your perspective.

Reflection Prompt:
How does it feel to let go of these old perfectionist messages? What would change if you practiced this new belief daily?

Early Recollections and Perfectionism
Let's talk about the magic of early recollections. During the first session with a client, Adlerian therapists always ask for an early recollection or memory. Typically, these memories will go back to around age five or six.

Early recollections are important indicators of an individual's personality dynamics and psychological development. These recollections reflect a person's perceptions and the meanings they made of certain events in their early life.

In therapy, we can analyze the early recollection and how an individual describes the memory to gain insight into a person's lifestyle, coping mechanisms, and beliefs.

Often, the client can identify and discover themes that weave through their early recollections and apply them to their current struggles. In the early recollections of a perfectionist, we may notice specific themes such as achievement and success, criticism and expectations, control and order, fear of failure, validation and approval, overachievement, and black-and-white thinking.

If you were to speak with a friend or a therapist, what would you tell them about how you are feeling and what your current struggles are related to perfectionism? Can you remember the first time you felt this way as a child? Get comfortable, close your eyes, take a deep breath, and go within to access these early feelings.

Exercise: Recalling Early Perfectionism
In detail, write down the earliest memory of this feeling as if you are writing a movie script.
- What themes do you notice?
- What is the most significant part of this memory that stands out the most to you?
- How did you feel at the time?
- How do you feel thinking about this memory now?
- Reflect on how these memories might have shaped your current perfectionistic behaviors.

The Fear of Disappointing Others
- How many of your childhood fears revolved around disappointing someone?
- Were you more afraid of failing or of letting people down?

Many perfectionists trace their first experiences of anxiety to a moment when they felt like they had fallen short.
- Maybe it was the first time you got a bad grade after always being the 'smart one.'
- Maybe it was missing a goal in a big game that made you feel like you let people down.
- Maybe it was your first failure in front of an audience, and the shame still lingers.

Pause for Reflection:
1. What is your earliest memory where you felt like you had to be perfect?
2. How did that moment shape how you see success and failure today?

Chapter Summary

In this chapter, we explored how childhood messages—spoken and unspoken—shape the standards you hold yourself to today. Whether you were taught to earn love through achievement, avoid mistakes at all costs, or always put others first, these early lessons formed the blueprint for your self-worth.

You learned how easy it is to carry those rules into adulthood without realizing it. Standards that once helped you feel safe or accepted may now fuel your perfectionism, self-doubt, or burnout. But seeing these patterns is the first step toward shifting them.

This isn't about blaming anyone. It's about understanding where your beliefs came from so you can choose new ones that reflect who you truly are, not just who you were taught to be.

In Chapter 6, Chase the Impossible Dream, we'll explore how these impossible standards evolve into a lifelong chase for approval, success, and certainty, and what it takes to step off that exhausting treadmill.

CHAPTER 6: CHASE THE IMPOSSIBLE DREAM

We don't suffer from life itself—we suffer from the imagined 'someday' ideals we attach to it.

In Adlerian psychology, this is called fictional finalism, the tendency to chase perfection in the hope that, one day, we'll finally feel enough.

The Illusion of the Perfect Future: Fictional Finalism and Perfectionism

Imagine you had a perfect life. The ideal job, the dream body, the unwavering success, the admiration of others. Maybe you've told yourself, *"Once I achieve _____ (success, wealth, love, recognition), I'll finally be happy."*

But here's the problem: whenever you get close to this imagined 'final destination,' the goal shifts further away.

This is the trap of fictional finalism, a concept developed by Alfred Adler to describe how we create unrealistic, imagined goals that we believe will finally bring us fulfillment. In Adlerian psychology, fictional finalism refers to the imagined future we believe will resolve all our struggles—a "final destination" where everything finally feels okay. But because this future is based on idealized expectations rather than reality, it stays just out of reach, fueling the inner treadmill of perfectionism. Instead of focusing on our present reality, we become fixated on an idealized version of ourselves that feels just out of reach.

Perfectionism's Trap: Why We Chase the Impossible

Perfectionists often impose idealized standards on themselves; they believe they will finally feel good enough if they reach a specific goal.

But the problem is that perfection is an illusion.

For example, imagine someone who starts a fitness journey with the belief: *"If I train daily, eat clean, and push myself, I'll look like a fitness model in three months."*

At first, they feel motivated. But when progress is slower than expected, frustration sets in. Instead of celebrating small wins, they fixate on how far they must go. This leads to self-doubt, exhaustion, and possibly giving up entirely.

Perfectionism shows up in many areas:
- **Career:** *"If I don't get this promotion, I'm not successful."*
- **Relationships:** *"I need to be the perfect partner, or I'll never be loved."*
- **Appearance:** *"If I don't look flawless, I'll be judged."*
- **Creativity:** *"If I can't create something perfect, why bother?"*

While focusing on desired outcomes and goals may seem healthy, problems arise when individuals cannot meet these high expectations. Instead of appreciating progress, they feel inadequate, reinforcing the belief that they are never 'enough.'

Adlerian Insight:
Adlerian psychology explains this as 'Striving for Superiority'—an instinct to grow, improve, and become better. However, this striving is fueled by fear rather than growth when perfectionism takes over. Instead of enjoying progress, the perfectionist sees only what's left to achieve. This concept explains our deep-seated need to grow, but it also shows how this instinct can turn into a perfectionist trap. Perfectionism isn't a high standard, it's a moving target. No matter how much we accomplish, the finish line keeps shifting, keeping us locked in a cycle of striving without satisfaction.

Now that we understand how perfectionism hijacks our natural drive for improvement, let's examine the specific fictional goals we've been pursuing.

The Perfectionist's Endless Race
Perfectionists often feel like they are running toward an invisible finish line—a dream of ultimate success that never quite arrives.

Does this sound familiar?
- *"If I just achieve this, I'll finally feel satisfied."*
- *"I'll rest once I prove myself."*
- *"I just need to get to this next level, and then I'll be happy."*

But what happens once the goal is reached?

The goalpost moves.

Instead of feeling a sense of peace and accomplishment, perfectionists immediately set their sights on something bigger, more challenging, and more unattainable.

Activity: Identify Your Fictional Goals

This activity will help you recognize the fictional goals driving your perfectionism.

Pause for Reflection:
Think of a goal you've recently reached.
Did it bring lasting peace—or did it quickly give way to the next thing on your list? What does that tell you about the way perfectionism frames your definition of success?

Let's take a moment to uncover some of these fictional goals.
- What perfect future are you striving for?
- Do you believe you'll finally feel happy, successful, or worthy once you reach this goal?

Write them down:
Example fictional goals:
- *"I must be highly successful to prove my worth."*
- *"I need to have the perfect relationship to feel loved."*
- *"Once I lose weight, I'll finally be happy."*

Now, reflect:
- How do these goals make you feel?
- Do they bring stress, anxiety, or a feeling of never being good enough?
- Do they help you grow or make you feel trapped in an endless chase?

Try to be as honest as possible during this activity. Identifying fictional goals does not mean you must abandon them completely; you can approach them without causing self-harm. Growth and progress take time. Change your inner narrative to allow for more kindness and less criticism.

Now that you've identified your fictional goals, let's challenge them.

Exercise: Rewrite the Narrative, Challenge Your Fictional Finalism
1. Pick one of your fictional goals.
2. Ask yourself:
   - What would realistically happen if things didn't turn out perfectly?
   - Would it be as bad as you fear?
   - Would you still be worthy, even if the outcome wasn't flawless?

Example:
Instead of *"I must be a best-selling author to be successful,"* try: *"I am still a writer even if my first book isn't a hit."* Success is a journey, not a one-time achievement."

A future-oriented mindset can fuel an unrelenting pursuit of excellence and contribute to constant failure and discouragement. Perfectionists may also be driven by fear of failure or falling short of their high standards. This fear can lead to excessive planning, procrastination, or avoidance of tasks perceived as challenging.

Case Study: Tess and The Artistic Perfectionist's Trap
Meet Tess.

She's a young woman with a passion for art and a dream of becoming a celebrated painter whose work hangs in galleries and inspires awe. She sees herself creating effortlessly, one masterpiece after another—her name, her work, her talent—recognized and revered.

Fueled by that vision, Tess buys the best supplies, sets up her studio, and finally sits down to paint. But as her brush hits the canvas, nothing feels right. The strokes feel clumsy. The colors clash. The image in her head refuses to come through her hands.

Frustration takes over. Her thoughts spiral:
"If I can't do this perfectly, maybe I'm not meant to do it at all."
Instead of pushing through the discomfort, Tess steps away. The canvas stays unfinished, and her brushes gather dust. Each time she walks past them, shame pricks at her.

She tells herself, *"Real artists don't struggle like this. If I had real talent, it wouldn't feel this hard."*

This is the perfectionist's trap. Tess didn't just want to paint—she wanted to be flawless from the start. Her focus wasn't on the joy of expression or the growth that comes through practice. It was in proving that she already was what she hoped to become.

And when reality didn't match her ideal, she gave up.
But here's what perfectionism didn't tell her: The path to mastery is always messy. The artists we admire have stacks of bad paintings behind every great one. What separates them isn't raw talent—it's the willingness to keep going.

If Tess had let herself be a beginner, she might've found her rhythm, her style. She might've fallen in love with the process instead of chasing the outcome. But perfectionism convinced her that struggle meant failure.

The truth? Struggle means you're in it. And staying in it is where growth—and greatness—begin.

Seeking Validation

Perfectionists often seek validation and approval from others to affirm their progress toward their fictional final goals of perfection.

Reflecting on the individual who started a workout routine may look to others for feedback on their appearance, such as losing weight or gaining strength. If they don't receive this validation, they might struggle to recognize their progress and accomplishments, leading to feelings of discouragement or failure.

Seeking validation can look like:
- Asking for reassurance that you're doing something 'right.'
- Measuring success by external praise instead of internal fulfillment.
- Feeling lost or unmotivated when no one acknowledges your progress.

Reflection Prompt:
Where do you seek validation in your life?
- How does it impact your self-esteem?
- Can you find ways to acknowledge your progress without relying on external approval?

Activity: Replace External Validation with Self-Affirmation

This reflection is about shifting the source of your worth—from something the world hands you, to something you already hold.

We know perfectionism thrives on approval. It feeds on praise, likes, gold stars, and nods of validation. But chasing that kind of worth is exhausting and fragile. This activity helps you build something more steady: a sense of self-worth that doesn't need permission.

Try this:
1. Name one place where you tend to seek validation.
   Example: *"I need others to compliment my work to feel I've done well."*
2. Write down how it feels when that validation doesn't come.
   Example: *"I start to question myself. I wonder if I've failed."*
3. Create a self-affirmation to speak back to that fear.
   Example: *"My work has value, even if no one applauds it. I trust what I bring."*
4. If you can, say your affirmation out loud daily. Let it interrupt the cycle. Let it land.

Reflection Prompt:
What would shift if your worth didn't hinge on anyone else's approval? How might you begin to trust your value, even in silence?

This chapter has asked hard questions—the kind that go deep into the stories you've lived. It's shown how perfectionism can keep you stuck in the loop of trying to prove, perform, and please. But it's also offered something more freeing: the idea that you don't have to keep chasing worth—you can start to reclaim it.

Chapter Summary

Perfectionism often promises that if you try hard enough, stay in control, and never mess up, you'll finally feel safe, worthy, and loved. But somewhere along the way, many of us start to realize that the finish line keeps moving.

This chapter mirrors the perfectionist's pursuit—one fueled by the need to prove, earn, and keep performing. We explored how this drive often masks deep fears: of being ordinary, of not belonging, of being found out. We named the cost—burnout, disconnection, anxiety, and the quiet grief of never feeling 'done.'

But you also began to see another possibility: that worth isn't something you chase. It's something you reclaim.

As we step into Chapter 7, Rewrite Your Inner Narrative, we'll begin to unpack what it means to be enough without the need to prove anything. You'll learn how to quiet the inner critic's voice and reconnect with a self that doesn't need to strive to deserve rest, love, or peace.

As you move forward, reflect on this:
What fear drives your perfectionism the most—fear of failure, rejection, or not being good enough?

Chapter 7 will help you break free from perfectionism's emotional grip and develop a healthier relationship with yourself.

PART III: CHALLENGE THE PERFECTIONIST MIND

Once we recognize our perfectionist tendencies and understand their origins, the next step is to challenge them. Adler argued that perfectionists often feel inferior, and instead of embracing growth, they try to overcompensate by proving their worth. But what if self-worth wasn't something you had to earn?

In Part III, we rewrite the perfectionist narrative by challenging old beliefs, embracing self-acceptance, and shifting from a fixed mindset to a growth mindset.

Chapter 7: Rewrite Your Inner Narrative— Changing how you speak to yourself.

Chapter 8: From Inferiority to Self-Acceptance— Understanding Adler's concept of inferiority and superiority.

Chapter 9: The Power of Connection— Moving from individual striving to social interest and belonging.

CHAPTER 7: REWRITE YOUR INNER NARRATIVE

Change how you speak to yourself.

When we measure our worth by how much we do, we begin to confuse productivity with significance. Adler teaches us that fulfillment doesn't come from doing more—it comes from belonging more.

This chapter is about that voice.
- The one that critiques your every move.
- The one that never lets you rest.
- The one you may have mistaken for truth.

It's time to start listening more closely—not to obey that voice but to understand it so you can change it.

Adlerian therapy teaches us that our personal narratives are not fixed—they are stories, and stories can be rewritten. We are not bound by the beliefs we formed in childhood; we can choose new ones that reflect who we are becoming, not just who we were taught to be.

The Perfectionist's Inner Critic: A Voice That Never Rests

Many perfectionists' inner dialogue is a constant stream of judgment and self-doubt.

Consider this:
- Would you say the things you say to yourself to a close friend?
- Would you expect someone else to meet the impossible standards you set for yourself?

Where does this inner critic come from?

- **Childhood Expectations:** If we are praised for being *"the smart one"* or *"the responsible one,"* we may feel pressure to maintain that identity at all costs.
- **Fear of Failure:** Many perfectionists developed their inner critic to avoid mistakes, believing they wouldn't disappoint others if they were hard enough on themselves.
- **Societal Pressures:** We live in a world that equates productivity with worth, making self-criticism necessary for success.

The Tricks of the Inner Critic: Cognitive Distortions in Perfectionism

The inner critic is not rational—it operates through cognitive distortions and exaggerated thinking patterns that convince us we are not enough.

Common Perfectionist Distortions:
All-or-nothing thinking – *"If I don't do it perfectly, I have completely failed."*
Reframe: *"Even if I make mistakes, I am still making progress."*

Catastrophizing – *"If I mess up, everything will fall apart."*
Reframe: *"One mistake does not define my entire success."*

Overgeneralization – *"I failed once, so I'll always fail."*
Reframe: *"Failure is a single event, not a lifelong pattern."*

Exercise: Identify Your Cognitive Distortions
1. Think of a negative thought that often shows up under pressure.
2. Identify the distortion behind it.
3. Write a more balanced, compassionate version.

This isn't about blind positivity. It's about finding a voice that's honest and kind within yourself.

When the Inner Critic Fuels Impostor Syndrome
Have you ever achieved something but still felt like a fraud?
Do you find yourself thinking, *"I don't deserve this success."*?

Impostor syndrome is when our inner critic convinces us that we are never genuinely competent, no matter how much we achieve or how hard we try. That quiet voice whispers, *"You don't belong here."* It's the nagging fear that your success is a fluke, that you're just pretending to be competent, and sooner or later, everyone will find out.

Even when you've worked hard, earned achievements, or received praise, impostor syndrome convinces you it's not enough. You downplay your strengths, credit luck or timing, and fear being 'found out.'

It's not a reflection of your ability—it's a distortion of your self-perception. And like perfectionism, it keeps you stuck in a cycle of overworking, self-doubt, and never feeling 'good enough.'

Impostor syndrome isn't about lacking success—it's about not letting yourself believe you've earned it.

Example: *"I only got this job because I got lucky."*
Reframe: *"I earned this opportunity through my work and experience."*

Pause for Reflection:
- Have you ever felt like you don't deserve your success?
- Have you ever explored where this belief comes from?

Now that we've explored how perfectionism shapes our inner dialogue, it's time to shift from simply recognizing these patterns to actively changing them. If you've ever caught yourself engaging in harsh self-criticism, feeling stuck in cycles of negative thinking, or struggling to accept your emotions, know that you're not alone. The good news? Just as perfectionist thinking is learned, it can also be unlearned. One of the most powerful tools in this process is self-compassion—the ability to speak to yourself with the same kindness and encouragement you would offer a dear friend.

The following exercises will help you recognize your inner dialogue, challenge negative self-talk, and practice accepting your emotions without judgment. These are not about 'thinking positive' in a forced way but rather about creating space for realistic, compassionate self-reflection. With time and consistency, you can train your mind to shift from self-criticism to self-acceptance, developing a healthier and more balanced inner narrative.

Compassion Isn't Weak—It's Healing

This chapter isn't about ignoring reality or forcing optimism. It's about learning to treat yourself like you treat others—with care, honesty, and grace.

Kindness isn't a detour from growth—it's the path that makes real transformation possible. Self-compassion isn't an excuse to stop striving; it's the foundation that helps you strive sustainably.

Perfectionists are often skilled at offering compassion outwardly, but inwardly? That's where the work begins.

You don't need to drown out the inner critic with false positivity. Instead, you can speak a little more truth and kindness into your day-to-day life.

Exercise: Replace Self-Deprecating Thoughts with Compassionate Ones
1. **List Three Negative Thoughts:**
   - Think of three negative thoughts you often have about yourself, especially in moments of stress or when you're feeling pressured to be perfect. Write them down.
   - **Example:** *"I'm not good enough," "I always mess things up,"* or *"I'll never be as successful as others."*
2. **Reframe with Compassion:**
   - Next to each negative thought, write a more compassionate and realistic version. Imagine you're speaking to a dear friend instead of yourself.
   - For instance, change *"I'm not good enough"* to *"I'm doing my best, and that is enough."* Or *"I always mess things up"* to *"Mistakes are part of learning; they don't define my worth."*
   - This practice helps you rewire your inner dialogue from criticism to compassion. It's not about forcing yourself to be overly optimistic but to cultivate a balanced and kind perspective.

Now that we've examined how to reframe negative self-talk with more compassionate alternatives, let's explore it further. Perfectionists often struggle with emotions they view as 'bad'—anger, jealousy, anxiety—when these feelings are natural and valid. The problem isn't the emotion itself; it's how we judge and suppress it.

The next exercise will help you acknowledge these emotions, making space for self-acceptance rather than resistance. By allowing yourself to feel without shame, you can break free from the cycle of self-rejection.

Exercise: Accept Your Feelings
1. **List Three Feelings You Don't Like:**
   - Think of three feelings you often wish you didn't have—anger, jealousy, or anxiety. Write them down.
   - **Example:** 'Anger,' 'Jealousy,' 'Anxiety.'
2. **Practice Acceptance:**
   - Next to each feeling, write a statement that acknowledges and accepts it without judgment. Use this format: *"Sometimes I feel [emotion], and that's okay. I accept myself with these feelings."*
   - **For example:** *"Sometimes I feel anger, and that's okay. I accept myself with this feeling."* or, *"Sometimes I feel jealous, and that's okay. It's a part of being human."*

The goal here is to practice accepting your emotions rather than trying to push them away or label them as 'bad.' Doing this creates space to explore what these feelings are trying to tell you.

Activity: Build a Daily Self-Compassion Habit
Objective:
This activity helps perfectionists create a daily practice of self-acceptance, reducing the power of their inner critic over time.

Instructions:
1. Identify a moment in your daily routine where you often experience self-criticism (e.g., morning mirror check, work deadlines, social interactions).
2. Write a self-compassion statement that directly counters your negative thoughts.
   - **Example:** Instead of *"I look awful today,"* try *"I don't have to be perfect to be worthy."*
3. Commit to saying this statement out loud (or in your head) daily during that moment.
4. Track your progress for a week. At the end of each day, write down how practicing self-compassion impacted your emotions and mindset.

Reflection Prompt:
What do you notice when you consistently speak to yourself with kindness? How does it change your self-perception?

Case Study: Learn to Rewrite Self-Talk
Meet Daniel.

Daniel was a high-achieving valedictorian, at the top of his class, and now works at a competitive firm. But no matter how much he accomplished, he felt like he was fooling everyone.
- When his boss praised him, he thought, *"They just don't see my weaknesses yet."*
- When he won an award, he told himself, *"It was just luck."*

The Turning Point:
One day, his mentor asked, *"Would you say those things to a friend?"*

Daniel realized he would never call a friend a fraud, so why was he treating himself that way?
- He started to recollect and record his achievements objectively.
- He practiced rewriting his self-talk from self-doubt to self-acknowledgment.
- Over time, his inner critic lost its power, and he finally felt deserving of his success

Chapter Summary
In this chapter, we turned inward, to the voice that shapes how you see yourself and show up in the world. You might have started to notice the patterns of your inner critic: the unrealistic standards, the quiet shame, the stories that have kept you in a loop of proof and performance.

You explored where that voice comes from—early expectations, fears, cultural pressure—and saw how perfectionism distorts your thought cycles through all-or-nothing beliefs, catastrophizing, and self-doubt. You also saw how those same patterns feed into impostor syndrome, convincing you that your success is a fluke and your confidence isn't real.

But more importantly, you started to shift the narrative. You practiced speaking to yourself with more compassion. You paused to question the harsh voice and chose to respond with something more honest and kind. You made space for feelings you were taught to reject. You took small but meaningful steps toward self-acceptance.

These shifts matter. They build the emotional foundation for what comes next.

In Chapter 8, From Inferiority to Self-Acceptance, we'll explore the deeper root of perfectionism, the quiet belief that you're not enough.

We'll help you uncover where that belief came from and how to let it go, so you can begin to live from a place of worthiness instead of performance.

As you move forward, consider this:
How does your fear of not being enough fuel your perfectionist tendencies?

Chapter 8 will help you break free from this fear and develop emotional resilience.

CHAPTER 8: FROM INFERIORITY TO SELF-ACCEPTANCE

Control can be a clever disguise for fear. The more tightly we grip, the more we reveal what we're afraid to lose.

Adlerian theory suggests that control is often an unconscious strategy to avoid vulnerability and reclaim a sense of superiority.

The Perfectionist's Struggle with Self-Worth

For perfectionists, self-worth often feels like something that must be earned.
- *"If I achieve enough, then I will feel worthy."*
- *"Once I am successful, I will finally accept myself."*

But no matter how much they accomplish, that feeling of inferiority never truly disappears.

Adlerian Insight:
Alfred Adler taught that feelings of inferiority are universal, but perfectionists believe they can erase them through achievement, validation, or comparison.

In this chapter, we will:
- Explore the origins of the inferiority complex and how it fuels perfectionism.
- Examine how comparison culture distorts self-worth.
- Develop strategies to embrace self-acceptance instead of seeking external validation.

It's time to stop proving your worth—and start believing in it.

Inferiority is a natural part of the human experience. We all have moments where we compare ourselves to others and feel like we don't measure up. However, what we do with those feelings determines whether they drive us forward or hold us back. Adlerian psychology distinguishes between healthy inferiority, which pushes us to grow, and an inferiority complex, which keeps us stuck in self-doubt and avoidance.

What exactly is an inferiority complex?

According to Adler, not all feelings of inferiority are bad. Healthy feelings of inferiority can drive personal growth.

Imagine you've always wanted to go to law school but haven't even started the applications yet. Then, you meet a new friend who has submitted her applications and received early acceptance. You start feeling inferior, thinking, *"Wow, I should've done this by now. She's ahead of me and even got accepted. I need to get moving."* These feelings can be a powerful motivator. Instead of spiraling into self-doubt, they push you to take action. You might even ask your friend how quickly she completed everything, which could give you the boost you need to get started. You could be working on your applications by the next day.

As the quote from An Anatomy of Jealousy, pg.12 says:

> *'The person who is content to do his best trusts others to accept and recognize the value of his contribution. He is able to live in contentment without tensions. He does not need to look to the right or to the left, and he is free to move forward without embarrassment in life.'*

On the other hand, an inferiority complex is when someone feels persistently inadequate or 'less than' others. These feelings often lead to low self-esteem and a lack of confidence. Take the same law school example: someone with an inferiority complex might think, *"I'm so lazy. I procrastinate all the time. I can't even fill out the applications. I'll probably mess it all up. Why bother? I'll never be as good as (insert name of friend here)."*

When someone feels like this, they might avoid taking action altogether. Their sense of inferiority becomes paralyzing. Interestingly, people struggling with an inferiority complex sometimes react by attempting to feel superior to others. Why? because it's a way of protecting themselves from those deep insecurities. By bringing others down—whether through judgment, control, or devaluation—they try to elevate themselves.

It's a defense mechanism that leads to unhealthy competition and jealousy. Adler believed that this kind of behavior undermines mental health and social interest, preventing people from forming genuine, supportive relationships.

Someone dealing with an inferiority complex may also swing toward feelings of superiority to feel more in control or better than others, which helps ease the pain of those deeper insecurities. If you're thinking, *"Why would someone who feels bad about themselves also feel superior?"* It's because, to feel better, they attempt to bring others down—judging, controlling, devaluing, or discrediting them—to elevate themselves. This creates a competitive, jealous dynamic that goes against what Adler saw as good mental health and social interest.

When an inferiority complex takes hold, it often fuels perfectionism. Instead of using feelings of inferiority as a motivation to grow, perfectionists try to compensate for their insecurities by setting impossibly high standards. The goal is no longer to improve but to prove they are never 'less than.' Let's explore how an inferiority complex fuels perfectionism and what we can do to break this cycle.

Pause for Reflection
Consider these questions as you reflect on your own experiences with inferiority:
- Can you recall a time when feelings of inferiority motivated you to take action?
- Have you ever experienced moments where those same feelings stopped you from trying?
- Do you ever notice yourself comparing your progress to others in a way that either motivates or discourages you?
- Have you ever caught yourself overcompensating by aiming for superiority? How did that affect your relationships with others?

The Inferiority Complex: How It Fuels Perfectionism
Why do perfectionists always feel 'not enough'?

Adler believed that every human experiences inferiority at some point in life. As children, we are small, dependent, and powerless, leading us to strive for growth, mastery, and approval.

But for perfectionists, this natural striving becomes an obsessive need to be the best, not for growth, but to eliminate self-doubt.
- Instead of striving to learn, they strive to prove.
- Instead of accepting their imperfections, they fear them.

The problem? Perfection can never erase feelings of inferiority—only self-acceptance can.

For many perfectionists, the need to feel 'enough' leads to an endless pursuit of success, status, and external validation. But what happens when this drive becomes unsustainable? The cost of prioritizing superiority can be far greater than we realize.

The Price of the Superiority Priority for Perfectionists

The downside for those prioritizing superiority is the constant pressure to maintain their 'plus' feeling. As the theory suggests, superiority-driven individuals often become overworked, tired, and stressed as they invest more and more energy into proving their worth. The 'price they pay' is exhaustion and burnout because they believe they will only maintain their sense of worth through continued achievement. In our society, which often values external success and achievement, perfectionists with a superiority priority may believe:
- *"If I am not the best, then I am nothing."*
- *"I need to work harder than anyone else to be valued."*
- *"I can't make mistakes because people will think I'm not good enough."*

This perfectionist mindset becomes a cycle of overworking and striving for unattainable goals, fueled by the fear of failure or not measuring up. While superiority is the most closely related to perfectionism, if you recall, other personality priorities manifest perfectionistic behaviors differently.
1. **Control:** Individuals who prioritize control feel most secure when they control their environment, tasks, or relationships. For a perfectionist with a control priority, life is about being in charge, organizing every detail, and avoiding unpredictability. They fear losing control, which may lead them to micromanage or avoid delegating tasks to others.
    - **Example:** A manager may insist on overseeing every aspect of a project to ensure it's done perfectly, believing that if anything goes wrong, they'll be blamed and feel incompetent.

2. **Comfort:** People with a comfort priority seek to avoid discomfort, stress, or difficulty. For perfectionists, this might mean avoiding tasks they think they can't excel at. They procrastinate or refuse to start projects because they fear they won't do them perfectly.
   - **Example:** A writer may delay starting a book because they're afraid it won't live up to the standard of other successful authors, which can cause them anxiety.
3. **Pleasing/Approval:** Those who prioritize pleasing want to be liked and approved by others. Perfectionists with this priority often overextend themselves to make others happy, believing that their worth is tied to the approval they receive from people around them.
   - **Example:** An employee might take on too much work or say 'yes' to everything, believing that if they don't, they'll let people down and lose their approval, reinforcing feelings of inferiority.

Understanding these different priority types gives us insight into how perfectionism manifests uniquely for each of us. The next step is shifting from a superiority-driven mindset to a healthier, more sustainable approach to self-worth.

Pause for Reflection: Recognize Your Inferiority Beliefs

1. When did you first feel 'not enough'?
   - Was it in childhood? School? Family expectations?
2. What messages did you internalize about success and failure growing up?
   - Were you praised only when you achieved?
3. What do you believe about yourself that may have started in those early experiences today?

Write down any thoughts or memories that arise—no judgment—just observation.

Now that we understand how inferiority drives perfectionism, let's take a moment to reflect on our personal experiences. The following activity will help you recognize the role of inferiority in your thoughts and behaviors.

Activity

- List and discuss moments where you have felt inferior or jealous of others.
- Identify whether these feelings were fleeting and motivational or persistent and debilitating.

Beyond recognizing moments of inferiority, it is important to explore how these emotions shape our relationships with success and others. Use the journal prompt below to reflect on your experiences with comparison and self-worth.

Journal Prompt

Has it ever been challenging to be happy for someone else's success? Sometimes, when someone else has succeeded in something we have not, their success feels like our failure. Have you ever experienced these feelings? You might think, *"How do I know if it's feelings of inferiority or an inferiority complex?"*

If you're unsure whether these feelings of inferiority are occasional or deeply ingrained, use this checklist to gain insight into your personal patterns.

Checklist Questionnaire: Do You Have a Secret Inferiority Complex?

Respond to the following statements with 'Often,' 'Sometimes,' 'Rarely,' or 'Never':

1. I criticize myself harshly and believe that my failures are due to my innate/inherent flaws.
2. I always need to appear perfect or boast about my achievements to feel valued.
3. I tend to withdraw from social situations where I might feel judged or vulnerable.
4. I experience physical symptoms like headaches or stomachaches when I'm stressed about my social image.
5. I avoid taking risks or trying new things because I fear I will fail.
6. I seek frequent reassurance or approval from others to feel good about myself.
7. I find it hard to feel genuinely happy for others when they succeed.

8. I often doubt my abilities and feel less competent or deserving than others.
9. I frequently compare myself unfavorably to my peers or colleagues.
10. I prefer to stick to tasks or activities where I am sure I will not fail or be judged.

Now that you have completed the checklist, reflect on your responses.

The following section will help you evaluate your thoughts and behaviors more fully.

Pause for Reflection
After reviewing your responses to the questions, please take a moment to reflect on them. If you identify with many of these statements, it might be a sign that an inferiority complex is influencing your thoughts and behaviors. This self-assessment can serve as a starting point for exploring these patterns further. Consider seeking additional support through professional guidance or alternative healing practices to work through these challenges.

Let's explore some of the common signs of an inferiority complex in greater detail.

11 Signs of An Inferiority Complex:
1. **Relentless Self-Criticism and Negative Self-Talk:** Criticizing yourself harshly or believing that your failures stem from inherent flaws rather than external circumstances.
2. **Overcompensating Behaviors:** Overcompensating for feelings of inferiority by striving for perfection, seeking attention, or boasting about your accomplishments.
3. **Social Withdrawal:** Avoid social situations where you feel vulnerable or fear judgment and rejection from others.
4. **Somatic Symptoms:** Experiencing anxiety, headaches, stomachaches, or other physical signs of stress related to concerns about your social image.
5. **Fear of Failure:** A deep fear of failure that prevents you from taking risks or stepping outside your comfort zone.

6. **Constant Need for Validation and Approval**: Seeking constant affirmation from others to feel good about yourself instead of trusting your worth.
7. **Difficulty Celebrating Others' Success**: It can be difficult to genuinely feel happy for others' achievements, often because their success highlights one's insecurities.
8. **Jealousy**: Feeling envious of others' successes and comparing yourself to them in a way that fuels unhealthy competition
9. **Constant Self-Doubt**: Frequently questioning your abilities and worth, feeling you're not as competent or deserving as others.
10. **Comparing Yourself to Others**: Habitually compare yourself to others and focus on your perceived shortcomings rather than your strengths.
11. **Avoidance of Challenges**: Staying in your comfort zone, avoiding new challenges or opportunities for fear of failure or judgment.

It is important to recognize how these patterns influence daily life and what they may signal about one's inner world.

Recognizing these signs can be the first step toward breaking free from the grip of an inferiority complex and moving toward healthier, more authentic growth and self-acceptance.

Recognize Where Jealousy Shows Up

- **Constant Self-Doubt**: Frequently questioning abilities, worth, or decisions, often doubting your competence or deservingness
- **Comparing Yourself to Others**: Habitually comparing yourself unfavorably to others, focusing on perceived shortcomings or deficiencies
- **Avoidance of Challenges**: People avoid taking on new challenges or opportunities for fear of failure or judgment and prefer to stay in their 'comfort zone.'

The Comparison Trap: Why Perfectionists Always Feel 'Less Than'

For perfectionists, self-worth is measured by comparison.

Do these thoughts sound familiar?
- *"I'll never be as successful as them."*
- *"Why does everything seem so easy for other people?"*
- *"I have to be the best, or I don't matter."*

Comparison creates a moving target because someone will always be ahead of you.
- If we tie our worth to external achievements, we are never truly free.
- The only way to break the cycle is to shift from external validation to internal self-acceptance.

Pause for Reflection: The Cost of Comparison
1. Who do you compare yourself to the most?
    - Are they people at work? On social media? Peers?
2. How does comparison make you feel?
    - Does it motivate you, or does it make you feel worse?
3. What if you measured yourself only by your growth, instead of someone else's achievements?

Reflect on one area of your life where comparison has kept you feeling 'not enough,' and consider what would change if you let go of it.

For many perfectionists, success is not a destination but a moving target. When they achieve one goal, they immediately focus on the next, never allowing themselves to truly feel satisfied. This cycle keeps them trapped in a state of 'almost enough'—where self-worth always feels just out of reach. Take a moment to reflect on whether you have been moving toward a fictional finish line.

Reflection Exercise: Do You Move the Finish Line?
1. Think of a significant goal you once dreamed about achieving.
    - Did it feel as satisfying as you imagined? Or did you quickly set another goal?

2. What happens when you accomplish something?
   - Do you allow yourself to feel proud? Or do you immediately focus on what's next?

Write down your answers. The aim of these questions is not to judge yourself, but to recognize patterns.

By recognizing these patterns, we can begin to shift our mindset. Self-worth isn't something to be earned—we cultivate it by acknowledging our progress, celebrating small victories, and allowing ourselves to experience pride without immediately chasing the next achievement.

The Cycle of Dissatisfaction

This mindset creates a cycle of dissatisfaction, where individuals never feel satisfied with their achievements because there is always another goal to pursue. You might set a significant goal for yourself, like getting a promotion or reaching a milestone in a personal project, and once you achieve it, you feel satisfied for a brief moment. But then, before you can truly appreciate your success, another goal comes along that leaves you feeling just as unfulfilled as before.

When the goal is always to reach the top, there is no ceiling, leaving many dissatisfied with their accomplishments and constantly searching for the next 'thing.'

By recognizing and challenging these fictional final goals—the idealized, often unattainable standards we set for ourselves—you can begin to cultivate healthier expectations and build greater self-compassion and self-worth. After all, isn't it reasonable to believe that we are inherently worthy of love and acceptance simply for being human, regardless of our accomplishments or perceived imperfections?

On a personal level, this is something I, Lindsay, have always struggled with. You'd think it would come naturally—to look in the mirror and accept yourself as attractive, even if not the next Mila Kunis or Gwyneth Paltrow. But for me, it hasn't been easy. I've battled with what I consider my most unforgiving imperfections: relentless cystic acne covering my face.

LIVING WELL WITH PERFECTIONISM

It's a cycle I know too well. There are a few 'good' days each month where my skin feels manageable, only to be followed by weeks of breakouts that no product or medication seems able to stop. I've spent countless hours searching for solutions—calling multiple dermatologists and rearranging my life to squeeze in a last-minute appointment. I've even found myself leaving work or skipping meetings, rushing to get injections that promise temporary relief. And when I walk out of the office, I breathe a small sigh of hope... but the weight of the issue always lingers.

This constant pursuit of perfection has been exhausting, even in something as personal and seemingly small as my skin. And yet, it's taught me something valuable. The more I chase flawless skin as the key to feeling 'enough,' the more I realize that it's not about the acne. It's about the belief that my worth is tied to my appearance—an idea that has kept me stuck in a cycle of striving and dissatisfaction.

Now that I'm a mom, this realization feels more critical than ever. I don't want my child to grow up thinking their worth is tied to their looks or accomplishments. I want to model self-compassion and show them that it's okay to have imperfections, make mistakes, and just be. I want them to know they are loved and worthy precisely as they are, and that starts with me believing it for myself.

Learning to break free from these fictional final goals isn't about giving up or pretending I don't care about my skin—it's about shifting my focus. Instead of obsessing over an impossible standard of perfection, I've started asking myself: *"What if I'm worthy of love and acceptance even on my 'bad' skin days? What if my imperfections don't define me but connect me to others who are struggling, too?"*

The truth is, real self-worth isn't found in flawless skin, a perfect body, or the next big accomplishment. It's found in accepting the messy, imperfect parts of ourselves and recognizing that they don't make us less—they make us human.

For anyone who feels trapped in a similar cycle, I hope this resonates: you don't need to earn your worth. It's already there, and we are waiting for you to acknowledge it. Letting go of perfectionism doesn't mean you stop caring; it means you start living. And maybe, just maybe, you find that you're not so imperfect after all. This constant striving sets the stage for the perfectionist trap, where instead of appreciating progress, we fixate on what's still missing. Let's take a closer look at why we keep chasing an impossible ideal.

Pause for Reflection

Determining your ultimate goal in life is not always straightforward. However, we can explore various areas of our lives to understand what is important to us and what we believe will lead us to a place of acceptance from ourselves and others. When we refer to acceptance from yourself and others, we mean what YOU BELIEVE will make you a worthy human being. You are worthy simply for being alive, yet we struggle to internalize this truth.

Lifestyle isn't just a goal; it's part of the journey. People often say, *"Once I have a nice car and a big house, I'll be happy,"* or *"Once I get that raise and promotion at work, I'll feel satisfied."* Was that enough for them?

We've explored how comparison can fuel feelings of inferiority. Let's look at a powerful Adlerian concept that helps us shift from this mindset. The 'Vertical and Horizontal Ladder' is a metaphor that illustrates two ways of viewing our relationships with others—one that keeps us stuck in comparison and one that encourages self-acceptance and growth.

The Vertical and Horizontal Ladder

Perfectionists often get stuck on a vertical ladder of comparison, constantly ranking themselves as either 'better' or 'worse' than those around them. This mindset fuels the cycle of inferiority and self-doubt.

In Adlerian psychology, the 'vertical and horizontal ladder' metaphor illustrates two different ways of viewing our relationships with others. The vertical ladder represents a hierarchical mindset, where individuals constantly compare themselves to others, seeing themselves as above or below them. This can lead to feelings of superiority or inferiority. In the case of an inferiority complex, a person may often feel stuck on the lower part of this ladder, always looking up at those they see as more successful or capable. To cope with this, they might try to climb higher by putting others down or striving to feel superior, hoping that this will make them feel more secure in their place.

On the other hand, the horizontal ladder represents a more balanced view, where people see themselves as equals, neither above nor below anyone else. Adler believed that proper mental health and social interest arise when we adopt this horizontal perspective. Instead of competing to be 'better' than others, we focus on cooperation, mutual respect, and contributing to the well-being of everyone around us. When we shift from the vertical to the horizontal ladder, we no longer feel the constant need to compare ourselves. This change allows us to embrace our strengths and imperfections without the pressure of constantly measuring up. By creating a sense of equality and community, we can move past the feelings of inadequacy that often feed an inferiority complex.

Case Study: Emily's Shift from the Vertical to the Horizontal Ladder
Let's talk about Emily.

She often felt stuck in a cycle of overwork and self-doubt. On the outside, she looked like a high achiever—always the first to take on extra projects and put in the hours. But no matter what she accomplished, it never felt like enough.

At work, Emily constantly compared herself to others. She immediately questioned her worth if someone else received praise or a promotion. *"Why can't I be as good as them?"* she'd think. So she pushed herself harder. But the harder she worked, the more isolated and drained she became.

In our sessions, we explored that pattern. Emily was viewing her life through what we called a "vertical ladder." On this ladder, she saw every situation as a ranking system—someone always above and below. Emily always felt near the bottom, looking up at the people she believed were better.

Her perfectionism was tied to that ladder. She believed that if she just climbed high enough, she'd finally feel good enough.

I introduced her to the idea of a different ladder—a horizontal one. Instead of ranking people, the horizontal ladder sees everyone standing side by side—not better, not worse—just human, each with strengths and flaws.

At first, this concept felt foreign to Emily, but we began with small shifts. When she felt anxious about a colleague's success, we paused to explore it. Could she see that person's win as a reminder that everyone—including her, had something valuable to offer?

Slowly, her question changed from *"How do I measure up?"* to *"What can I contribute?"*

With time, things began to shift. Emily no longer needed to be better than everyone else to feel valuable. She let go of the pressure to climb and focused on how she could show up with presence and purpose. She became more connected to her colleagues, accepting of her imperfections, and grounded in her worth.

It didn't happen overnight. But eventually, Emily stepped off the endless climb toward perfection. In its place, she found a steadier, more balanced sense of self—one not built on comparison, but on connection.

If you see yourself in Emily's story, you're not alone.
The good news? You don't have to stay on the vertical ladder. The shift begins with awareness, and with practice, you can change the way you see yourself and the people around you.

Exercise: Step Off the Ladder

If Emily's story resonated with you, this exercise is your invitation to shift from comparison to connection, from striving to self-worth.

Let's explore how the 'vertical ladder' might be showing up in your own life—and how to move toward something healthier.

1. **Notice the Moment**
   Think back to a recent situation where you felt not enough. Maybe it happened at work when a colleague got praised. Or during a family conversation when someone seemed to have it all together. Or even scrolling through social media.
   - What thoughts came up in that moment?
   - Were you comparing yourself? Judging yourself? Trying to prove something?

   Write down what you remember.

2. **Draw Your Ladder**
   Grab a blank piece of paper. Draw a simple vertical ladder.
   Now place yourself on it—where did you feel you stood in that moment?
   - *"Below my colleague who got the promotion."*
   - *"Not as good as the mom who always has it together."*
   - *"Behind everyone else in my field."*

   Then ask yourself: How did being on that ladder make you feel? Motivated? Deflated? Anxious? Disconnected?

3. **Flip the Ladder**
   Now draw a horizontal line. Place the people from that same situation side by side with yourself.
   Instead of seeing them as above or below, identify what each person brings, including you.
   - *"She's confident in meetings—I'm thoughtful and detailed."*
   - *"He's quick to act—I'm steady under pressure."*

   No one is better. Just different. And that's okay.

4. **Reframe the Thought**
   Take a breath. Ask yourself:
   - What shifts when I see others as peers, not competitors?
   - What happens when I stop ranking and start recognizing?

   Write down one or two new thoughts you can return to when you catch yourself climbing the vertical ladder again.
   Examples:
   - *"I'm not behind—I'm on my own path."*
   - *"We each bring something valuable."*
   - "I don't need to be the best to be enough."

5. **Practice the Shift**
   For the next week, stay aware of your ladder moments.
   When you notice yourself comparing, pause. Picture that horizontal line. Say your new thought out loud (or silently), and see what changes—inside and out.
   Keep a journal if it helps. Not to be perfect about it—but to track how it feels to step off the climb, and step more fully into yourself.

Looking Within: The Worth Equation
In a quiet moment, consider what makes you feel valued or valuable. Does your sense of worth depend on external achievements? Notice when you feel most confident versus when you doubt yourself.

Try this: Imagine losing your job title, awards, or accomplishments overnight. Would something of you remain worthy? This isn't about diminishing your achievements but about discovering what lies beneath them.

If you're comfortable, journal about a time when you felt worthy despite not "earning" it through achievement.

The Difference Between Self-Worth & Self-Esteem
Self-Esteem = Based on performance, success, and comparison.
Self-Worth = Unconditional, based on 'being' rather than 'doing'.

The key to self-acceptance? Stop chasing self-esteem—and start embracing self-worth.

Activity: The Self-Acceptance Mirror
Step 1: Write down three things you value about yourself unrelated to achievement.
- **Example:** *"I am kind," "I care deeply," "I am creative."*

Step 2: Say them out loud in front of a mirror.
- Notice how it feels—do you believe these statements, or do they feel uncomfortable?

Step 3: Repeat this exercise daily.
- The more we practice seeing ourselves beyond achievements, the easier self-acceptance becomes.

At first, it might seem strange to validate yourself, but the transformation is impossible to miss when you start to do this habitually. You are your biggest cheerleader. It's normal to need time to get comfortable with this idea. Stick with it; this will become easier with time.

Reframe Inferiority: The Path to Self-Acceptance

Instead of chasing perfection, what if you embraced imperfection?

Self-acceptance does not mean giving up on growth—it means recognizing that you are already enough while you grow.

Perfection says, *"I need to be flawless to be worthy."*
Self-acceptance says: *"I am worthy exactly as I am."*

Adlerian Insight:
Adler believed that true self-acceptance comes from recognizing that our worth is inherent, not something to be earned.

Exercise: Your Personal Inferiority Story
Objective:
This journaling exercise helps you explore your relationship with inferiority, perfectionism, and self-worth. By writing about these experiences, you can gain clarity, process emotions, and shift your mindset toward self-acceptance.

Instructions:
1. Think back to your earliest memory of feeling inferior.
    - What happened?
    - How did it make you feel?
    - Did this experience shape how you view success, failure, or self-worth today?
2. Identify a recent moment when you felt 'not enough.'
    - What triggered this feeling?
    - What thoughts ran through your mind?
    - How did you react?
3. Now, rewrite your story.
    - If you could go back and speak to your younger self in that first memory, what would you say?
    - If you could reframe your recent self-doubt, how would you talk to yourself with kindness instead?
    - What new beliefs about self-worth would you like to adopt moving forward?

Final Thought:
Take a moment to recognize how past experiences have shaped your self-worth. This will allow you to rewrite your narrative with self-compassion. Let this exercise be a step toward releasing the need to prove yourself and embracing the truth that you are already enough.

Chapter Summary

In this chapter, you explored one of the deepest roots of perfectionism: the quiet belief that you're not enough.

We looked at how feelings of inferiority, often shaped early in life, can drive perfectionist behavior. You may not walk around thinking, "I'm inferior," but you might feel it when you compare, when you can't rest, and when you believe success is the only way to prove your worth.

You met Emily and saw how easy it is to get stuck climbing a vertical ladder—constantly measuring yourself against others, always trying to get to the top. And you saw what's possible when you shift to a horizontal view: one where you can stand beside others, not above or below them.

You practiced accepting emotions you were taught to judge—anxiety, anger, jealousy—as part of being human, not signs that you're flawed. You explored the possibility of letting go of comparison and choosing self-worth that isn't tied to performance.

This work isn't always comfortable. But it's necessary. Because freedom from perfectionism doesn't come from reaching the top of the ladder—it comes from stepping off it entirely.

In Chapter 9, The Power of Connection, we move from inner healing to outward expression—what it means to be seen without the mask of perfection. You've done the hard work of challenging your inner critic and confronting the belief that you are not enough. Now comes the deeper invitation: to let others in.

CHAPTER 9: THE POWER OF CONNECTION

In trying to be everything for everyone, we forget what it feels like to be ourselves.

Adlerian theory invites us to rediscover significance through genuine connection, not people-pleasing.

We don't need perfect people. We need present ones.

We spend so much energy trying to earn our place—at work, in relationships, even in our own lives. But true belonging doesn't require performance. It asks you to be real.

If perfectionism taught you to hide the messy parts of yourself, connection invites you to bring them to the table. The parts you once feared might push others away are often the very things that draw people closer.

This chapter is about unlearning the belief that you must be flawless to be loved. It's about building relationships that hold space for your full humanity—the strong, the soft, the striving, and the still-in-progress.

The Hidden Loneliness of Perfectionism

You walk into a room full of people, smiling and nodding, but inside, you feel entirely alone. You have built walls—walls of success, control, and perfection. But instead of bringing you closer to others, those walls have only trapped you inside your mind.

At its core, perfectionism is about control, the belief that if we can just be perfect enough, achieve enough, or avoid mistakes, we will be worthy of love and acceptance.

But perfectionism doesn't lead to deeper connections—it creates loneliness.

- Do you find yourself putting on a 'perfect' mask in relationships?
- Do you struggle to ask for help, fearing it will make you look weak?
- Do you avoid vulnerability because you fear judgment?

Adlerian Insight:
Alfred Adler believed that our psychological well-being is deeply connected to our sense of belonging. Humans are social beings, and our greatest fulfillment comes from genuine relationships.

The irony? Perfectionists often struggle the most with connection because they fear being truly seen.

In this chapter, we will:
- Explore why perfectionism fuels disconnection and loneliness.
- Understand how relationships can help us overcome self-doubt.
- Learn how to practice vulnerability and cultivate authentic connections.

It's time to shift from trying to prove our worth to allowing ourselves to be seen.

Perfectionism doesn't just show up in one area of life—it seeps into our work, relationships, and even leisure activities. We create idealized versions of what life 'should' look like, and when reality doesn't match up, we feel disappointed. But have you ever stopped to examine what your vision of 'perfection' actually looks like?

Your Vision of 'Perfection' in Key Life Areas

What do you envision for your future in these life tasks? What is your 'perfect' scenario? How does chasing these fictional goals feed into your perfectionism? Does it lead to procrastination, fearing that your efforts won't be 'perfect'? Or does it push you to overwork yourself to achieve flawless outcomes?

- Work
- Friendship
- Love/Romance
- Leisure/Hobbies

How does this impact your current goals? On a scale from 1 to 5 (one being the lowest and five the highest), how satisfied are you in these areas? What could help you achieve one point higher in each?

Pause for Reflection
1. Take a moment to think about your own fictional goals. Have you ever set a goal for yourself that felt 'perfect' but was ultimately unattainable?
2. Did you find yourself seeking approval from others to feel validated?
3. Write down an example of when you felt driven to pursue perfection, only to be left unfulfilled.

By recognizing how perfectionism influences our expectations in these areas, we can begin making adjustments that allow for more flexibility, self-compassion, and fulfillment. Instead of striving for an unattainable ideal, we can shift toward setting meaningful, realistic goals that align with our values, not just external validation.

The Isolation Trap: When Perfection Builds Walls
- *"If they saw the real me, they wouldn't stay."*
- *"I don't want to be a burden."*
- *"I just need to keep it together."*

These are the quiet beliefs that build emotional walls. They don't always sound dramatic. They sound reasonable, even responsible. But they keep you alone.

Perfectionism doesn't just demand performance—it discourages connection. There's no room to be known when you're trying so hard to be impressive.

You may find yourself keeping relationships on the surface. Being helpful, funny, and polished—but never quite letting people in. You might avoid asking for help, not because you don't need it, but because needing feels like failing. And while the world sees someone competent and in control, you're carrying the weight of never feeling seen.

Here's the paradox: We chase perfection to feel worthy of connection. But it's our vulnerability, not our performance, that brings people closest.

Perfection says, *"Don't show your flaws—you'll be judged."*
Belonging says, *"You don't have to be more. Just be real."*

True belonging doesn't come from being flawless. It comes from being honest. And honesty includes receiving—not just giving. For perfectionists, it can feel safer to offer support than to ask for it. But real connection is mutual. Letting others help you isn't weakness—it's trust.

Case Study: Maya and the Mask of Independence

Maya was the strong one. The capable one. The one everyone went to for advice, for help, for getting things done.

At work, she ran teams with precision. At home, she held everything together. Her calendar was full, her standards were high, and her emotions? Neatly tucked away.

She didn't see herself as a perfectionist—just someone who 'got things done.' But in therapy, she admitted something she rarely voiced:

"I don't think anyone really knows me. I don't even know if I'd let them."

Maya wasn't just tired—she was lonely. She had built her life around competence, but deep down, she longed for connection,
real connection, the kind that would allow her to stop holding it all together.

Through reflection and gentle challenges, she started to experiment. A small confession to a friend. A missed deadline she didn't beat herself up over. A moment where she said, *"I can't do this alone."*

The response? No rejection. No shame. Just warmth. Understanding. Relief.

Maya didn't collapse when she let go of the mask. She softened. And for the first time in a long time, she felt like she belonged—not because she was flawless, but because she was real.

Pause for Reflection:
1. Do you ever feel you need to 'earn' love and acceptance?
   - What are some ways you try to prove your worth in relationships?
2. How comfortable are you being vulnerable?
   - Do you share your struggles with others or keep them hidden?
3. What do you believe would happen if you let people see the real you?
   - Would they reject you, or would they accept you as you are?

Write down your thoughts. The goal is not to judge yourself but to recognize patterns.

When perfectionism takes hold, it often turns our focus inward—toward our flaws, our image, our performance. But Alfred Adler believed our psychological well-being is deeply connected to our sense of belonging. He called this *social interest*—our ability to feel part of something larger, to contribute, and to care about the well-being of others. This outward shift, from proving to participating, is where healing begins. When we contribute to others, we naturally build self-worth, resilience, and meaningful connections.

Cultivate Social Interest and Empathy

When someone is perfectionistic, they often focus inwardly, thinking about themselves. Adler believed that the cure for many mental issues was to help individuals develop social interest and concern for their community and fellow human beings. Shifting from inward-focused perfectionist tendencies to outward-looking, empathetic, and socially engaged behaviors is important. When someone doesn't feel good about themselves, doing something to help others can make them feel much better.

We must feel we are valuable members of society, as if we count and have something important to contribute. I can use my 4-year-old 'middle child' of four children as an example. Without getting into too much detail about all the kids, you can imagine being in the middle with older siblings who are excelling and a cute baby brother. It can be hard to find significance. Rafa learned he can scream, have tantrums, sing loudly, and fill in the blanks for annoying acts and other misbehaviors. In this case,

Rafa is very self-focused in his toddler's mind. If we turn to Adler, he suggests we get Rafa involved in helping somehow- direct him toward the useful side of life. For example, at dinner, if he starts to 'act out,' instead of reprimanding, punishing, or arguing with him, I might suggest he helps me set the table or pour the drinks for everyone. Maybe I'd even ask him to feed the baby. The same concepts can apply to us as adults when we are very concerned with ourselves.

Next, we will explore practical exercises and reflective practices designed to instill social interest, a healthier mindset, and more fulfilling connections.

Adler's concept of social interest, or the German word **Gemeinschaftsgefuhl** (which has a whole book written about its meaning!), suggests that a sense of belonging and contributing to the welfare of others can significantly reduce perfectionist tendencies. By focusing on the community and engaging in acts of kindness, individuals can shift from self-centered perfectionism to a more balanced and fulfilling perspective.

Pause for Reflection: How Does Perfectionism Affect Your Relationships?

1. Do you struggle to ask for help or let people see your struggles?
   - If yes, what do you fear will happen?
2. Do you feel you must 'perform' in relationships instead of being your true self?
   - In which relationships do you feel safest? Why?
3. How might your perfectionism be keeping you from deeper connections?

Write down your reflections and notice any recurring patterns.

Developing social interest isn't just a theoretical concept—we can actively cultivate it through intentional actions. The following exercises will help you strengthen your connection to your community and reinforce your empathy by engaging with others meaningfully.

Exercises and Activities to Practice Purposeful Connection
Community Connection Map:
Purpose:
To visualize and strengthen your connections within the community.

Activity:
Draw a map with places you frequently interact with others, such as your neighborhood, workplace, school, or local cafe. Note the type of interactions you have and identify areas where you could increase your involvement or improve the quality of your interactions.

Reflection:
Consider how you can contribute positively to these spaces and plan specific actions.

Impact Circle Mapping
Generate a purpose

Activity:
Draw concentric circles representing different community layers (family, friends, work, local community) around a 'me' center. Note your contributions and potential for positive impact in each area.

'A Day in Their Shoes' Journaling:
Purpose:
To develop empathy and understand diverse perspectives within your community.

Activity:
Choose someone from your community map. Spend a day observing or imagining life from their perspective—Journal about the experience, focusing on the insights gained about their challenges and joys.

Reflection:
Reflect on how this experience might change your interactions or perceptions of others in your community.

Community Improvement Project:
Purpose:
To actively contribute to the betterment of your community.

Activity:
Identify a need within your community that resonates with you. This could be anything from starting a community garden to organizing a neighborhood clean-up to setting up a free book exchange. Plan and execute the project with the help of neighbors or community members.

Reflection:
Document the project's progress and outcome versus the process.

By incorporating these exercises into daily life, we begin shifting away from self-focused perfectionism and toward a healthier, community-driven mindset. In the next section, we will explore how social engagement leads to deeper personal fulfillment and reduces the pressures of perfectionism.

Break the Wall: Embrace Vulnerability in Relationships
What if being seen for who I really am doesn't push people away, but brings them closer?

Many perfectionists consider vulnerability a risk, but it is the foundation of genuine connection.

The antidote to perfectionism is not more control—it is courage.
- Courage to show up imperfectly.
- Courage to ask for help.
- Courage to let yourself be seen, flaws and all.

Challenge: The Small Acts of Vulnerability Ladder
Vulnerability is like a muscle—the more we use it, the stronger it gets.

If sharing our imperfections feels terrifying, the key is to start small and build up gradually.

Instructions:
1. **Start With The 'Safest' Act Of Vulnerability**
   - Tell a trusted friend about a small mistake you made recently.
   - **Example:** *"I messed up my schedule this week and forgot an important call."*
   - Notice their reaction—did they reject you or empathize?

2. **Level Up: Share an insecurity with someone you trust**
   - Open up about a personal struggle—something you'd usually keep to yourself.

   Example: *"I've been feeling really overwhelmed lately, and I put so much pressure on myself to get everything right."*

3. **Take It Public: Allow yourself to be seen in imperfection**
   - Let yourself be imperfect in a social setting.

   Example:
   - Admit you don't know something at work.
   - Post something online without over-editing it.
   - Show up to a gathering without feeling the need to impress.

4. **Reflect on your experience**
   - What happened?
   - Did anyone reject you, or did they relate to you more?
   - How did it feel to be honest instead of 'perfect'?

The more we normalize imperfection, the less power perfectionism has.

Pause for Reflection: Let Yourself Be Seen

Think back to a moment when you let your guard down—when you shared something real with someone you trust. Maybe it was a quiet confession, a tearful truth, or a moment when you finally said, *"I'm not okay."*

- How did they respond?
- Did it bring you closer? Did you feel more known, more understood?

Now ask yourself: What gets in the way of that kind of honesty?
- Are you afraid of being judged, rejected, or misunderstood?
- Do you ever worry that showing your real self might make others pull away?

And finally, who in your life feels safe?
- Who listens without trying to fix you?
- Who sees you, even when you're not at your best?
- What might it look like to lean into that connection?

Take a moment to write down what comes up—not to analyze it, but to notice. The more honest you are with yourself here, the more space you create for real connection.

How Genuine Connection Creates Self-Acceptance
What if the best way to silence your inner critic was not through achievements but relationships?

Adlerian Insight:
Adler believed that self-acceptance is developed in the community. When we surround ourselves with people who accept us without conditions, we begin to accept ourselves in the same way.
- Healthy relationships remind us that we are worthy, just as we are.
- Authentic connection helps us shift from external validation to internal self-worth.
- Being seen and loved despite our imperfections is the ultimate cure for perfectionism.

Pause for Reflection: Who Are You Letting In?
The way we see ourselves is often shaped by the people closest to us, sometimes in ways we don't even realize.

Take a moment to reflect:
- Who has influenced how you value or question your worth? Have their words lifted you, or chipped away at your self-belief?
- Which relationships make you feel the most seen and accepted? How might you nurture those connections a little more intentionally?
- And what kind of support do you need right now? Have you let anyone know?

Write down one small action you can take this week to strengthen a relationship that matters to you. Not a grand gesture. Just something honest, human, and real.

Sometimes, connection doesn't begin with others showing up for us—it starts when we let them in.

Chapter Summary:

In this chapter, we explored the quiet loneliness that so often hides behind perfectionism. You began to see how striving to appear flawless can create distance between you and others—and how that distance frequently gets mistaken for strength, when really, it's fear dressed up in control.

We talked about masks—the ones we wear to avoid judgment and the ones we forget we're even wearing. But we also looked at what happens when we begin to let others see who we really are—not the polished version, the real one—the one that's tired, hopeful, messy, and still worthy.

You learned how connection doesn't come from impressing people. It comes from letting them in. It comes from vulnerability—the courage to be seen in your imperfection. Because when we stop performing and start showing up as we are, something powerful happens: we're met with love, not rejection.

We also explored how Adler's concept of *social interest* can gently shift our focus outward, from self-doubt to contribution, from isolation to belonging. When we engage with others meaningfully, we start to remember that we matter—not because we're perfect, but because we're connected.

In Chapter 10, Balance Work, Love, and Community, we'll explore how to live a more integrated life, one where your values, your relationships, and your sense of self work together, not against each other. This next chapter is about building a life that fits, not one you constantly have to prove yourself in.

What if the way to truly connect with others is to first connect with yourself?

Let's find out.

PART IV: BUILD A BALANCED LIFE

Perfectionists struggle with balance. They feel pulled between success and relationships, work and well-being, productivity and rest. Adler emphasized the three life tasks—work, love, and community—as essential for mental health and happiness. When one area dominates the others, we feel unfulfilled.

In Part IV, we redefine success beyond perfectionism and learn how to build a life rooted in harmony, purpose, and human connection.

Chapter 10: Balance Work, Love, and Community— Adler's three life tasks and how to balance them.

Chapter 11: The Present Moment as Your Refuge from Perfectionism— How presence quietly disarms perfectionism.

Chapter 12: Your New Best Friend, Your Inner Cheerleader— Shifting from self-criticism to self-encouragement.

CHAPTER 10: BALANCE WORK, LOVE, AND COMMUNITY

A balanced life isn't one where nothing tilts — it's one where everything gets to matter.

Adler identified work, love, and community as the three life tasks of adulthood — not to perfect, but to live meaningfully.

We often think of balance as something delicate and impossible to maintain, like walking a tightrope. But maybe it's not about perfect distribution at all. Maybe balance simply means making space for what matters.

The Balancing Act of a Fulfilled Life
For many perfectionists, balance feels like an impossible dream. Work, relationships, and personal well-being always seem to suffer.
- *"If I focus on my career, my relationships take a hit."*
- *"If I prioritize my relationships, I feel like I'm falling behind professionally."*
- *"If I take time for myself, I feel guilty for not being productive."*

Does this sound familiar? Perfectionists tend to excel in one area while feeling like they are failing in another. The pressure to be the best at everything leads to overcommitment, burnout, and emotional exhaustion.
- But what if the balance wasn't about juggling everything perfectly?
- What if balance meant being present, intentional, and aligned with what truly matters?

Adlerian Insight:
Alfred Adler believed a meaningful life is built on three key life tasks: work, love, and community. He argued that fulfillment doesn't come from perfect balance, but from intentional integration, where we show up with presence, not pressure.

These three areas aren't just categories; they are the canvas of a full life.

In this chapter, we will:
- Explore why perfectionists struggle to balance work, relationships, and community involvement.
- Redefine balance as a flexible, evolving practice, not a fixed destination.
- Develop practical strategies to create harmony in all areas of life.

It's time to stop 'doing it all' and step into a life that feels whole and meaningful.

The Perfectionist's Struggle with Integration
Meet Jenna.

For years, Jenna was the ultimate high achiever. She worked 70-hour weeks, constantly pushing for the next promotion. Friends invited her out, but she was too busy. Her family wanted to see her, but she was too exhausted.

"I'll make time once I reach the next milestone," she told herself.

But when she finally got the promotion, she felt... nothing.

Her relationships had faded, and she had no energy for her passions. The success she had worked so hard for felt hollow.
- This is what happens when work overshadows love and community.
- Perfectionists chase achievement at the cost of connection and feel empty.

Are you sacrificing relationships for success? Or neglecting personal fulfillment because of work?

From Exhaustion to Alignment: The Shift Toward Balance
For many perfectionists, the struggle with balance is not about not knowing what matters—it's about not feeling allowed to prioritize what matters.

- We know relationships are essential, but convince ourselves to invest in them later.
- We know we need rest, but feel guilty when we take it.
- We know life is about more than work, but we still let work dictate our self-worth.

The real issue isn't time, it's permission.

What if the balance wasn't about perfect scheduling but permitting yourself to be human?

Shifting from burnout to balance starts with these realizations:
- Balance doesn't mean equal time—it means aligned priorities.
- Slowing down doesn't mean falling behind—it means choosing what truly matters.
- True success isn't about external validation but inner fulfillment.

Perfectionism says, *"I'll make time for what matters later."*
Balance says, *"Later is now."*

Now, let's explore why perfectionists struggle to slow down—and how to break free from the cycle.

Why Perfectionists Fear Slowing Down
Why do perfectionists feel guilty when they step back?
The perfectionist's core fear:
- *"If I slow down, I'll fall behind."*
- *"If I stop working so hard, I'll be seen as lazy."*
- *"If I don't give 110%, I won't be successful."*

But here's the truth:
- Rest is not failure.
- Prioritizing relationships doesn't make you weak.
- Success doesn't disappear when you create balance.

Adlerian Insight:
Adler emphasized that life satisfaction is tied to personal fulfillment, not external success. Perfectionists often confuse busyness with meaning, but the true meaning comes from purpose, connection, and balance.

What Happens When We Never Slow Down?

- **Burnout:** Constantly pushing for perfection leads to exhaustion, cynicism, and detachment.
- **Loneliness:** Work replaces relationships, and success starts to feel empty.
- **Loss of Joy:** Hobbies, creativity, and simple pleasures become 'unproductive' distractions.
- **Health Consequences:** Chronic stress leads to anxiety, sleep issues, and even physical illness.

You might still look like you're succeeding. But inside, you're running on empty.

We often fear slowing down, without realizing that not slowing down costs us everything we truly want.

Reframe Productivity: Rest is a Power Move

Perfectionism says, *"Slowing down is weakness."*
Reality says, *"Slowing down is a strategy."*

Highly successful people understand that:
- Rest fuels performance.
- Time off creates clarity.
- Personal fulfillment leads to better work, not less.

What if stepping back wasn't a failure, but the very thing that made you stronger?

Let's stop fearing balance—and start embracing it, one honest adjustment at a time.

The Three Pillars of a Fulfilling Life

Adlerian Insight:

Adler believed that life is most fulfilling when we integrate three essential life tasks:

Work: Purpose and Contribution

- Work is not just about money or achievement—purpose, creativity, and impact.
- Perfectionists often tie their identity to work, making it their primary measure of success.

Reframing Work:

- Work should support your life, not consume it.
- Your job is what you do, not who you are.

Love: Deep, Meaningful Relationships

- Love includes romantic relationships, friendships, and family bonds.
- Perfectionists often struggle with vulnerability in relationships, fearing rejection, judgment, or loss of control.

Reframing Love:

- Love isn't something to master—it's something to experience.
- You don't have to be perfect to be worthy of connection.

Community: Belonging Beyond Yourself

- Community includes friendships, mentorship, social involvement, and contributing to something bigger.
- Perfectionists often see community as secondary to work and relationships, but a strong sense of community provides support, perspective, and purpose.

Reframing Community:

- You don't have to 'earn' your place in a community.
- Belonging is about showing up as you are, not proving your worth.

How would your life feel different if you valued all three areas equally?

Pause for Reflection: Are You Balanced?
1. Which of the three pillars—work, love, or community—feels the strongest in your life?
2. Which pillar do you feel you are neglecting the most?
3. What is a straightforward step this week to nurture that area?

Write down a small, achievable action to create more balance.

Exercise: How to Realign Your Priorities
If perfectionism has pulled you out of balance, this activity will help you gently recalibrate. You don't need to overhaul your entire life—you need to start noticing where your time and energy are going, and where your values are being left behind.
Let's look at your week with fresh eyes.

Step 1: Take Inventory
Look back at the last 7 days and ask yourself:
- How many hours did I spend on work or tasks related to achievement?
- How much quality time did I spend with people I care about?
- Did I make space for hobbies, rest, or community involvement?

Be honest, not judgmental. This isn't about assigning blame—it's about seeing the patterns.

Step 2: Find the Imbalance
Which one of Adler's three life tasks—Work, Love, and Community—is getting the most of your energy?

Which one is being neglected?

Sometimes, we overcommit in one area because it feels easier to control, or because our perfectionism tells us it's the only one that really matters. But imbalance leads to burnout, disconnection, and emptiness.

Step 3: Make One Small Shift
You don't need a radical change. Just a rebalancing move—one small adjustment that brings your life a little closer to what matters most.

Try something like:
- **If work dominates:** Schedule protected time for something joyful or restorative, such as coffee with a friend, a walk, or time off your phone.
- **If love feels distant:** Reach out to someone you care about, share something real, and make space for connection.
- **If community is lacking:** Do one small thing that connects you to something bigger than yourself—volunteer, offer support, or simply show up where you're needed.

Write it down
- What's your small shift this week?
- Write it out as a commitment to yourself: *"This week, I will..."*

Let it be doable. Let it be honest. And let it be a reminder: balance isn't a destination. It's a practice of coming back to what matters—again and again.

Now that you've assessed where your time and energy go, reflect on the broader picture of your lifestyle choices. This next exercise will help you explore how your personal preferences, challenges, and habits influence your overall balance.

Pause for Reflection: What Does Your Life Reflect?

List your current lifestyle choices: Where do you work? Who do you hang out with? What do you do for fun or leisure? Do you have a romantic partner or date? What is your love life like right now?
- What aspects of life come quickly to you?
- What tasks do you find more challenging?
- What activities and tasks do you gravitate toward, and which do you prefer to avoid? (Please answer for each life task listed below.)

Life Tasks:
- Work/Career
- Social/Community (friends, neighborhood, etc.)
- Intimate Relationships (romantic relationships, sex, marriage, etc.)

Journal Prompt
Do your current lifestyle choices bring you genuine satisfaction, or do perfectionist standards primarily drive them? What are the consequences of striving for perfection in these areas of your life? How do you feel when you fall short of your perfectionist expectations? Are there any benefits or drawbacks to your perfectionistic tendencies?

The Importance of Community
Adler believed that human fulfillment is deeply connected to community involvement.

What does this mean for perfectionists?
- Community provides perspective. It reminds us that we are not alone in our struggles.
- Service gives meaning. When we contribute to something beyond ourselves, we find a deeper purpose.
- Belonging heals perfectionism. When we feel accepted, we stop tying our worth to achievement.

Community isn't a luxury; it's a necessity.

How can you reconnect with your community? Volunteering, friendships, mentorship?

Create Integration: Small Shifts, Big Impact
Meet Tom.

Tom was a workaholic for years—until a major health scare forced him to re-evaluate his priorities.

"I realized I had spent my life working but neglected the people I loved. I wasn't even sure who I was outside of my job."

Slowly, he made minor changes:
- Leaving work on time to spend more time with family.
- Scheduling weekly coffee dates with friends.
- Finding joy in hobbies, not just work achievements.

Tom didn't become less driven—he stopped driving himself into the ground. He started building a life, not just a résumé.

What slight shift can you make today to allow more balance into your life?

For so long, perfectionism may have made you believe that your worth is tied to how well you perform, how flawless you appear, or how much you achieve.

However, true belonging is not a result of perfection; it comes from being authentic and honest with yourself.

Chapter Summary:

This chapter wasn't about doing more—it was about doing differently. You've spent so much of your life trying to manage everything—pushing harder, performing better, reaching higher. But if you're honest, that constant striving hasn't always brought you peace. It caused pressure, exhaustion, the quiet ache of wondering if you're missing what matters most.

We explored how perfectionism often knocks our lives out of alignment. We end up overinvesting in one area, like work, while neglecting the others that feed our sense of purpose: love and community. Through the lens of Adler's three life tasks, you learned how to redefine balance, not as perfect time management but as living in tune with what truly matters.

You've seen that success isn't just a job title. It's connection, contribution, and presence. And balance isn't about getting it all right—it's about giving yourself permission to show up as a whole human being.

In Chapter 11: Live in the Present, Let Go of the Past, we'll explore how perfectionism keeps us either stuck in what was or terrified of what's ahead. You'll learn how mindfulness—simple presence—can pull you out of overthinking and help you land in the only place where real life happens: right here, right now.

Let's step off the treadmill of proving—and into the life that's already waiting for us. Wholeness doesn't mean equal energy everywhere. It means enough presence where it matters.

CHAPTER 11: THE PRESENT MOMENT AS YOUR REFUGE FROM PERFECTIONISM

Worth is not something you earn; it's something you uncover.

Adler saw self-esteem not as ego, but as the courage to be imperfect while still contributing to the world.

Where Are You Right Now?

Perfectionists are rarely fully present. Their minds are always racing ahead, planning, analyzing, striving, and anticipating.

- *"What if I fail?"*
- *"What's the next step?"*
- *"I have to be prepared for every possibility."*

But in all this future-thinking, one thing gets lost: **the present moment.**

For perfectionists, 'now' often feels like something to endure rather than experience. The mind is always somewhere else, trying to control, fix, or plan.

But what if presence, not perfection, was the real key to peace?

Adlerian Insight:

Alfred Adler emphasized the importance of living with social interest and engagement in the here and now. He believed that fulfillment is not found in striving for a perfect future but in being fully connected to our present experiences.

Adler also believed courage is not the absence of fear, but the willingness to show up as we are, especially when we feel imperfect.

In that way, mindfulness becomes more than a technique—it becomes a courageous act. It's how we stop outsourcing our worth to the future and begin trusting ourselves in the present.

In this chapter, we will:
- Explore why perfectionists struggle to stay present.
- Understand how perfectionism fuels time anxiety and hypervigilance.
- Learn how mindfulness can break the perfectionism cycle.
- Develop practical grounding techniques to embrace the now.

It's time to stop racing ahead and start living fully—right here, right now.

The Perfectionist's Hypervigilance: Always Scanning for 'What's Next'

Do you feel like you are always living for the next thing?

Perfectionists tend to live in three mental time zones:
- **The Future:** *"I'll be happy when I achieve this."*
- **The Past:** *"I should have done that differently."*
- **The Present** (but not really): *"I'm here but thinking about what's next."*

This is the time trap of perfectionism—where the mind rushes ahead or clings to the past, never fully engaging in the moment.

This hypervigilance isn't just about planning—it's about scanning for failure, anticipating mistakes, and fearing the unknown.
- *"What if I say the wrong thing?"*
- *"What if I fail and everyone sees?"*
- *"What if I don't prepare enough and it goes badly?"*

What's the cost?
- Chronic stress.
- Difficulty enjoying small moments.
- Always feeling behind, no matter what's achieved.

What if success wasn't about what happens next? How fully would you experience it now?

For many perfectionists, daily life feels like an endless cycle of tasks, deadlines, and expectations. The joy of being present gets lost in the rush toward the next achievement. But what if we shifted our mindset from focusing on results to embracing the process?

One common issue we often hear from clients is the challenge of not feeling 'present' throughout their days and not thoroughly enjoying life. This struggle is familiar to many due to busy schedules and distractions like smartphones, technology, to-do lists, and social media. The end goal can become our sole focus when we become primarily outcome-oriented. Adding tasks to our to-do lists, no matter how small, can make success feel only achievable when we can cross them off. However, these lists are often never-ending for those leading busy lives.

I often use the example of laundry. As a wife and mom to four children, doing laundry is a never-ending process. I used to have weekly mental battles over wanting the laundry baskets empty, with all the clothes folded and put away. It didn't feel very encouraging when the baskets quickly filled up again after finishing the task. It was like being on a StairMaster—continuously stepping but getting nowhere!

It became more manageable when I accepted that laundry is an ongoing task without a definite end and began to focus on what I enjoyed about the process. We can apply this same idea to other ongoing activities in our lives.

For instance, consider this workbook we're writing. As recovering perfectionists, we've talked for years about creating it, but it was never the 'perfect' time. We often found reasons why it wouldn't be good enough or why we shouldn't do it. Finally, as professionals who help others tackle perfectionism, we decided to take 'messy action.' Once we began writing, we wanted to finish it in one night to reach the end goal—a finished workbook in hand!

However, this mindset can be discouraging since completing a project like this takes time. Instead, we started focusing on the process itself. What do we enjoy about writing? What can we learn? What do others stand to gain along the way? Even if this workbook was never finished, could we still benefit from the process of creating it? The answer is yes. The process has tremendous benefits, not just for us but also for our clients, friends, and community.

We continue to share what we learn, and writing itself is rewarding. It's essential to embrace the process and dare to engage, even if it doesn't go exactly as planned.

There's a documentary called *"Cave Digger"* about a man named Ra Paulette, who digs massive sandstone caves in New Mexico as art. Wealthy patrons pay him to create caves that become beautiful, intricate works of art. He uses only hand tools for this process, which can take several years to complete. One cave he had been working on for a few years suddenly collapsed. He remained completely calm when he went to tell the person who hired him about the collapse. The person was shocked and asked how he could be so calm after his hard work was destroyed. He replied that he loves what he does and appreciates the process of digging and sculpting the caves. He knows the cave could collapse, but still dedicates time to all the small details and difficult labor. Reframing how we approach our daily tasks can help us experience a greater sense of presence and fulfillment. Rather than measuring success by completed checklists, we can focus on how each moment shapes our personal growth. The following section will explore practical exercises for staying present and letting go of perfectionist pressure.

Pause for Reflection: How Much Do You Live in the Future?
1. Do you spend more time thinking about the future than experiencing the present?
2. When did you last pause and notice where you were?
3. What would open up for you if you didn't spend so much time anticipating the next thing?

Write down your thoughts. Awareness is the first step toward breaking free from future-based anxiety.

Mindfulness: The Art of Being Where You Are
Mindfulness is the antidote to perfectionism.

What is mindfulness?
- It is not about emptying the mind—it's about being fully engaged in the present.
- It is paying attention without judgment.
- It is choosing to be where you are instead of being lost in what-ifs.

Why is mindfulness powerful for perfectionists?
- It interrupts overthinking.
- It trains the mind to focus on one moment at a time.
- It reduces stress by shifting attention to the now.

Trust grows where presence is practiced. The more you anchor into the now, the more you reinforce the belief that you can handle life—not perfectly, but presently.

Learning to Trust the Present Moment
Meet Tori.

Tori used to plan everything—her career, relationships, even how she would spend weekends a month in advance.

"If I could just control everything, I'd feel safe."

But the more she planned, the more anxious she felt. Instead of giving her control, her obsession with the future robbed her of peace.

One day, a friend asked: *"What would happen if you let yourself be where you are?"*

At first, Tori resisted. Slowing down felt impossible. But slowly, she began practicing mindfulness techniques—breathing, noticing, and engaging with the moment.

The result? For the first time, she felt genuinely present.
- Now, instead of asking, *"What's next?"* she asks, *"What's now?"*

What would shift if you trusted the present moment instead of fearing the unknown?

Activity: The 'Now Experiment' – Practicing Presence in Daily Life
The Experiment:
Step 1: Choose one activity to experience today fully.
- Pick an activity you usually rush through, multitask, or do on autopilot.
- Examples: Drinking coffee, showering, driving, or eating a meal.

Step 2: Set a clear intention to be fully present.
- For this activity, commit to experiencing every part of it.
- Pay attention to each sensation, movement, and sound, without distraction.

Step 3: Notice when your mind wanders, then gently return.
- It's normal for the mind to drift into planning, worrying, or analyzing.
- When you catch this happening, acknowledge it and return to the experience.

Step 4: Reflect on how it felt.
- Did you feel more relaxed?
- Did the experience feel richer or different from usual?
- How often do you engage in the present like this?

This experiment allows you to break the cycle of mindlessly moving through life, helping you experience what it feels like to be present.

Incorporating mindful behaviors into daily life can help us break free from rigid thought patterns. One way to make this process engaging and interactive is through a simple yet effective tool: Adlerian Bingo. This activity reinforces self-awareness, compassion, and connection to others, enjoyably and practically.

Exercise: Adlerian Bingo
Adlerian Bingo Card:
Carry this card with you throughout the week and mark a square each time you perform or recognize one of the listed behaviors. Aim to complete a line horizontally, vertically, or diagonally to achieve 'Bingo.' At the end of the week, reflect on your experiences to evaluate the impact of these behaviors on your perceptions and interactions.

LIVING WELL WITH PERFECTIONISM

B	I	N	G	O
Gave a genuine compliment	Accepted a flaw without judgment	Asked for help when needed	Choose cooperation over competition	Noticed and corrected a negative thought
Shared a personal mistake	Felt genuine happiness for another's success	Took a risk despite the fear of failure	Encouraged someone to be their authentic self	Listened actively without planning a response
FREE (Courage to be imperfect)	Reflected on a past success	Acted despite feeling inferior	Offered help without being asked	Felt connected to a community
Set a realistic goal.	Acknowledged a limitation without self-judgment	Spent time on personal reflection	Said no to an unrealistic demand	Celebrated a small win
Learned something new without striving for mastery	Forgave someone's mistake	Enjoyed a moment without trying to perfect it	Implemented a small change	Prioritized personal well-being over productivity

Instructions for Using the Adlerian Bingo Card:
1. **Mark the Square:** Each time you do, or even witness, one of these actions, mark it off.
2. **Aim for Bingo:** Complete a row, column, or diagonal line by the end of the week.
3. **Reflect on Your Experiences:** At the end of the week, consider the following questions to deepen your understanding of how these behaviors influence your approach to perfectionism:
   - Which actions were most straightforward for you to achieve and why?
   - Which squares were challenging to complete? What does this reveal about your habits or mindset?
   - How did focusing on these behaviors affect your week, especially your feelings and interactions?
   - How can you consistently incorporate these positive behaviors into your daily routine?

Completing this exercise may reveal patterns in your thinking and behaviors. Now, let's take a moment to self-reflect—who are you without your achievements?

Pause for Reflection: Who Are You Without Your Achievements?
1. What happens when you are not being 'productive'—do you feel restless, guilty, or uncomfortable?
2. If no one were watching, if there was nothing to 'achieve' today, what would you do just because you enjoy it?
3. What does this reveal about how much of your worth is tied to what you do rather than who you are?

Notice what comes up. If it feels tender or uncomfortable, that's not a problem—it's the beginning of change.

Chapter Summary:
Perfectionists struggle to stay present because they constantly focus on what's next or what went wrong. The need to plan, anticipate, and avoid mistakes keeps them locked in cycles of stress and self-judgment. In this chapter, we explored how perfectionism fuels time anxiety and how mindfulness relieves the pressure to always do more.

Through real-life stories, self-reflective exercises, and grounding techniques, we uncovered the power of being where you are rather than where you think you should be. We introduced 'The Now Experiment' to practice presence in daily life and Adlerian Bingo to make mindfulness an interactive habit.

Perfectionists can experience greater inner peace, clarity, and self-compassion by shifting from achievement-based self-worth to presence-based fulfillment.

Key Takeaway: Perfectionism keeps you chasing an impossible future, but the life you want is happening right now.

Now that we've explored how to slow down and be present, the next step is shifting how we speak to ourselves.
- Perfectionists have a loud inner critic—but what if you replaced that voice with an inner cheerleader?
- What if instead of tearing yourself down, you learned to encourage yourself the way you would a friend?

In Chapter 12, Your New Best Friend: Your Inner Cheerleader, we'll explore how self-compassion can replace self-judgment, rewiring how you see yourself, from flawed and never enough to worthy and growing.

Let's meet your inner cheerleader.

CHAPTER 12: YOUR NEW BEST FRIEND, YOUR INNER CHEERLEADER

Limits don't shrink our worth — they reveal our wisdom.

To Adler, embracing reality doesn't mean giving up. It means living with courage, not an illusion.

If your inner critic has been running the show, this chapter is your turning point. It's time to meet the voice inside you that doesn't demand perfection, but cheers for progress. The one who sees your effort, honors your humanity, and reminds you that you're doing better than you think.

The Voice in Your Head

There's a voice inside your mind that narrates everything you do.

For perfectionists, this voice isn't always kind.
- *"You should have done that better."*
- *"Why can't you just get it right?"*
- *"If you fail, people will think you're a fraud."*

This is the inner critic, the voice that tells you that you're not enough, no matter how much you accomplish.

But what if this voice could be different?

What if, instead of tearing you down, it cheered you on?

Adlerian Insight:

Alfred Adler believed that early experiences and social comparison shape self-worth. If we internalize the belief that we are only valuable when we achieve, we develop an inner critic that punishes us for not being perfect.

- The good news? This voice is not permanent.
- You can rewire it to replace your inner critic with an inner cheerleader.

The goal isn't to silence the inner critic—it's to **transform** it. In Adlerian therapy, this is called re-education: we gently teach ourselves new beliefs, grounded not in fear or perfectionism, but in encouragement and truth. Your inner voice can evolve, not by force, but by practice, patience, and compassion.

Recognizing our inner critic is the first step, but the fundamental transformation happens when we replace self-judgment with self-compassion and encouragement. Let's explore how shifting from praise to encouragement can fundamentally change how we see ourselves.

Self-Compassion and Encouragement

Self-compassion and encouragement are crucial steps in healing from perfectionism. Adlerian psychology emphasizes the importance of treating ourselves with kindness and understanding, recognizing our shared humanity, and encouraging ourselves and others. There is a significant difference between praise and encouragement in Adlerian psychology. Praise typically involves acknowledging and admiring specific achievements or qualities in a person. For example, a child brings home a picture they colored, and the parent says, *"Wow, that picture is excellent! You are a good drawer"*. This statement would be considered praise, like *"good job"* or *"good girl,"* because it focuses on the outcome or result, often reinforcing a sense of superiority or comparison.

Sometimes, we see parents comparing children to their siblings- *"Why can't you be a good boy like your brother?" "Look at Sally; she is sitting and being a good girl."* When we say someone is 'good,' we may consider that if they're not good, they must be bad, and children will look for this kind of praise to test if they are 'good' or 'bad.' Telling someone, *"You are the smartest kid in the class,"* might feel pretty good, but what happens when they don't get the best grade? Will that child still feel good? Will they receive the same praise?

On the other hand, encouragement in Adlerian psychology emphasizes the process, effort, and improvement rather than the result.

Encouragement aims to nurture individuals' sense of competence and capability by focusing on their actions and progress, regardless of the outcome. For example, if a child brings home coloring that is not perfectly drawn inside the lines, a parent may say, *"Wow, I see you must have spent a lot of time working on this. I love how you selected so many colors for his shirt-you must have put a lot of thought into that!"*.

Encouragement motivates individuals to strive for personal growth and development rather than competing with others. For example, if someone gets a low grade on a test despite their best effort and hours of studying, the teacher or parents may say, *"I appreciate the effort you put into studying. You gave your best effort on that exam."*

From an Adlerian perspective, praise can sometimes lead to feelings of superiority or inferiority because it is easy to rely on external validation. Encouragement creates a sense of intrinsic motivation and self-worth, promoting individuals' belief in overcoming challenges and pursuing their goals autonomously. Encouragement is genuinely a skill and an art, with entire books and courses devoted to its teaching. With that said, we may not be able to count on receiving encouragement from others regularly, but we can learn to encourage ourselves. This chapter will guide you through exercises to promote a compassionate inner dialogue and an encouraging attitude.

It is important to note that many clients who come to us have struggled with standard therapeutic techniques such as Cognitive Behavioral Therapy (CBT). CBT is one of the most empirically supported and frequently used modalities in modern counseling, with substantial research demonstrating its effectiveness across various mental health conditions, including depression and anxiety (BPS Medicine, 2021). However, despite CBT's reputation as a powerful tool for self-improvement, it can fall short for some people. Many clients find that, even though they attempt to alter their thought patterns and have the logical capacity to do so, they struggle to internalize these changes entirely. This challenge is widespread among perfectionists, who often delve even deeper into self-criticism in their pursuit of flawless thinking. This can lead to frustration, as they question why cognitive distortions persist despite their awareness and understanding of the process.

The real difficulty lies in balancing the acknowledgment and validation of emotions while simultaneously scrutinizing one's thoughts and feelings for potential distortions—a process that can be incredibly challenging for those prone to self-criticism.

As we shift from external validation to self-encouragement, we create a more resilient and compassionate internal dialogue. The following section will explore practical exercises to reinforce this mindset and build an inner voice that truly supports us.

Why Self-Compassion is Not Complacency

Many perfectionists fear that they'll lose motivation if they stop criticizing themselves.

Reality check:
Research by Dr. Kristin Neff shows that self-compassion leads to higher motivation, not lower.

To encourage yourself doesn't mean accepting mediocrity but fueling growth without burnout.

Ask yourself:
"Has self-criticism ever made me feel energized long-term, or just exhausted?"

Exercise: Self-Acceptance Letter Writing Exercise & Creative Expression for Imperfection

Deepening the Technique:
Writing a self-acceptance letter is a powerful exercise in Adlerian therapy that nurtures self-compassion and challenges perfectionist tendencies. It's about acknowledging and accepting your flaws, mistakes, and all aspects of your being with kindness.

Steps to Enhance the Technique:
Step 1: Preparation
- Find a quiet and comfortable space where you can reflect without interruptions.
- Consider the tone you want to set for the letter. It should feel like it's coming from a supportive and understanding friend.

Step 2: Writing the letter:
- Start with Self-Reflection: Acknowledge your feelings about your imperfections and the pressure you put on yourself to be perfect.
- Forgiveness: Move to forgiving yourself for times when perfectionism has led to self-criticism or missed opportunities for enjoyment.
- Affirmation of Strengths: Highlight your strengths and qualities unrelated to achievements or perfection. Affirm your value beyond your productivity or accomplishments.
- Commitment to Growth: Conclude by committing to continue working on accepting your imperfections and growing from them rather than letting them be a source of self-reproach.

Step 3: After writing:
- Read Aloud: Read the letter out loud to yourself in a compassionate tone. Hearing the words can make them more powerful and affirming.
- Store or Display: Keep the letter where you can see or access it easily. Some people find it helpful to read their letters regularly, especially when they feel critical of themselves.

Step 4: Share (optional):
- Sharing the letter with a therapist, friend, or support group can be incredibly validating. It reinforces your commitment to self-acceptance and encourages others to engage in similar reflective exercises.

A Personal Story from The Author.

I didn't realize how much my inner critic controlled me for years. I believed that being hard on myself was what kept me successful.
- If I made a mistake, my inner voice immediately scolded me.
- If I succeeded, my inner voice moved the goalpost.
- If I rested, my inner voice whispered that I was falling behind.

I remember one particular moment that made me truly aware of how loud my inner critic had become. I had just finished a major project that took months of work.

By all accounts, it was a success—I received positive feedback, people were congratulating me, and yet, I felt nothing but anxiety. My first thought wasn't, *'I did a great job.'* It was, *'I should have done more. I should have started earlier. I should have worked harder.'* That night, I lay in bed, replaying every tiny thing I could have done better instead of allowing myself even a moment of satisfaction.

I realized then that I had spent years achieving but never actually feeling accomplished. The voice in my head wasn't helping me—it was punishing me. No matter what I did, I could never meet its impossible standards. It wasn't until I started actively questioning my thoughts that I understood my deeply ingrained self-criticism.

The turning point came when I imagined saying those words to someone I loved. Would I ever look at a friend who had just completed something meaningful and say, *'You should have done more. You didn't work hard enough. You're still not good enough?'* The thought was horrifying. And yet, this was how I spoke to myself every single day.

That's when I decided: If I wouldn't say it to someone I cared about, I wouldn't say it to myself. The first time I tried shifting my inner dialogue, it felt foreign, like I was speaking a language I didn't know. But little by little, I replaced *'You should have done better'* with *'You did your best, and that's enough.'* I started treating myself with the same kindness I gave to others. And slowly, the voice in my head softened.

I thought I was motivating myself, but I was exhausting myself.

One day, I asked myself:
"Would I ever talk to a friend this way?"

The answer was no.
- If a friend were struggling, I would encourage them, not punish them.
- So why did I treat myself differently?

That was the turning point. I decided that if I wouldn't speak this way to a friend, I wouldn't talk this way to myself.

And that's when everything changed.

What if you spoke to yourself like you would to someone you loved?

If you struggle with perfectionism, you might have noticed that no achievement ever seems to be enough. When you reach one goal, a new one takes its place, keeping happiness just out of reach.

This cycle is what Alfred Adler called fictional finalism—the belief that we'll finally feel worthy and fulfilled once we reach a certain point. But this is an illusion.

Let's look at how this plays out in our daily lives.

Case Study: The 'Good Enough' Breakthrough
Meet Maria.

She was the type who would rewrite an email five times before sending it.

One day, she tried a challenge: Sending something at 80% instead of 100%.
- Instead of rereading and overthinking, she hit 'send.'
- Instead of regret, she felt… relief.
- Nothing terrible happened—no one even noticed the 'imperfections.'

That moment shifted everything for Maria. She realized she had been spending hours perfecting things already good enough.

Reflection:
What is one area where you can try 80% effort instead of 100%?

Activity: Identifying Your Fictional Goals
This activity will help you recognize the fictional goals driving your perfectionism.

Let's take a moment to uncover some of these fictional goals.
- What perfect future are you striving for?
- Do you believe you'll finally feel happy, successful, or worthy once you reach this goal?

Write them down:
Example fictional goals:
- *"I must be highly successful to prove my worth."*
- *"I need to have the perfect relationship to feel loved."*
- *"Once I lose weight, I'll finally be happy."*

Now, reflect: How do these goals make you feel?

Do they bring stress, anxiety, or a feeling of never being good enough?

Are they helping you grow or making you feel trapped in an endless chase?

Now that you've identified your fictional goals, take a moment to reflect: Are these goals truly serving you? Or are they making happiness feel like something you can only reach 'someday'?

The key to living well with perfectionism isn't about chasing an idealized version of yourself; it's about learning to accept where you are right now.

Now that you've identified your fictional goals, let's challenge them.

Activity: Challenge Your Fictional Finalism
Rewriting the Narrative
Pick one of your fictional goals.

Ask yourself: What would realistically happen if things didn't turn out 'perfectly'?

Would it be as bad as you fear?

Would you still be worthy, even if the outcome wasn't flawless?

Example:
Instead of *"I must be a best-selling author to be successful,"* try: *"I am still a writer even if my first book isn't a hit. Success is a journey, not a one-time achievement."*

A future-oriented mindset can fuel an unrelenting pursuit of excellence and contribute to feelings of constant failure and discouragement. Perfectionists may also be driven by fear of failure or falling short of their high standards.

This fear can lead to excessive planning, procrastination, or avoidance of tasks perceived as challenging.

For instance, let's take the example of Tess, a young woman passionate about art. She dreams of becoming a celebrated painter whose work will be admired in galleries worldwide.
She envisions herself effortlessly creating masterpiece after masterpiece, her talent recognized and revered.

Fueled by this vision, Tess buys the finest supplies, sets up a studio, and dives into her first painting. But as she works, she finds her brushstrokes clumsy, her colors mismatched, and her composition far from the masterpiece she imagined. Frustration sets in. Tess starts thinking, *"If I can't create something amazing immediately, maybe I'm just not cut out for this."*

Instead of continuing to practice and learn, she abandons the painting. Her brushes start to gather dust as they lie on a shelf, untouched. Every time she walks past them, she feels a pain run through her body of failure. She tells herself, *"Real artists don't struggle like this. If I had real talent, it wouldn't feel this hard."*

This is a common trap for perfectionists. Tess imposed an idealized standard on herself, producing gallery-worthy art from the start. Her focus wasn't on the joy of learning or expressing herself but on achieving a flawless outcome. When reality didn't align with her expectations, she gave up entirely, leaving her dream unfulfilled.

The path to success, whether in art, fitness, or any pursuit, is rarely linear or immediate. Progress often comes from messy, imperfect attempts that lead to growth over time. By letting go of rigid expectations and embracing the learning process, we create space for our dreams to evolve in ways we might never have imagined.

Had Tess kept painting despite her frustration, she might have discovered her unique style and built the skills to achieve her goals. But she allowed perfectionism to dictate her worth, forgetting that greatness is born out of perseverance, not instant mastery.

As we see in Tess's story, perfectionism often convinces us that anything less than flawless isn't worth doing. But true success isn't about reaching an impossible ideal—it's about learning, evolving, and allowing yourself to grow at your own pace. Let's explore how you can shift your mindset from perfection to progress.

Let's take a step toward redefining success. The following exercise will help you set goals that align with your values rather than perfectionist pressures.

Activity: Reframing Immediate Desires into Growth Journeys
1. **Immediate Desires vs. Long-Term Goals:** List your immediate desires ('be') and describe what the journey to achieving these ('become') might involve.
2. **Identifying Steps:** Break down the 'become' journey into smaller, achievable steps, noting the learning and milestones involved for each step.
3. **Reflection:** Reflect on how shifting from a 'be' to a 'become' mindset changes your feelings toward your goals. Does it reduce pressure? Empower you to act?

Exercise: SMART Goal Setting for Perfectionists:
Transform perfectionist goals into SMART (Specific, Measurable, Achievable, Relevant, Time-bound) goals, focusing on effort, learning, and progress rather than perfection.

Activity: Reframe 'Being' vs. 'Becoming' Exercise
Journey Log:
Keep a log of your journey toward a significant goal. Note challenges, lessons, and victories.

Growth Milestones: Identify and celebrate each step of progress, no matter how small, like learning a new skill or conquering a fear.

Seeking Validation
Perfectionists often seek validation from others to affirm their progress toward their fictional final goals of perfection. Reflecting on the individual who started a workout routine, they may look to others for feedback on their appearance, such as losing weight or gaining strength.

If they don't receive this validation, they might struggle to recognize their progress and accomplishments, leading to feelings of discouragement or failure.

Adlerian Definition: Fictional Finalism

Fictional finalism is "the individual's unconscious, subjectively conceived, ever-present goal of success—the self-ideal."

In other words, think of fictional finalism as a mental picture of your 'ideal self'—a version you believe you must become to feel worthy, satisfied, or complete. It's a personal, often unconscious goal we chase to feel successful. You might tell yourself, *"Once I achieve ___ (success, wealth, recognition), I'll finally be happy."* But the reality is that this goal often feels out of reach, and when you get close, it shifts even further away.

The Childhood Origins of Fictional Finalism

Think back to when you were a child. What did you tell yourself about the future?

- *"Someday, when I grow up, I'll be famous, and then people will love me."*
- *"Once I get straight A's, my parents will be proud."*
- *"If I look perfect, I'll be admired."*

As children, we naturally develop idealized versions of ourselves. These fictional final goals aren't always opposing—they can motivate us to work toward success. But when our self-worth becomes tied to achieving these unrealistic standards, we become trapped in an endless cycle of perfectionism.

These goals/standards often start in childhood, where we create an image of who we need to become to feel good about ourselves. You might remember saying to yourself, *"Someday, when I grow up..."* This childhood belief is an early form of fictional finalism, where we believe the future holds the key to our happiness. As adults, this morphs into new forms, such as *"Only when I am ___ (good, rich, skinny, important, successful, in control) will I feel ___ (admired, accepted, secure, significant)."*

Often, we chase after a fictional goal—an ideal version of 'perfection' that we believe will bring us happiness or success. This future-oriented mindset can fuel an unrelenting pursuit of excellence and contribute to feelings of constant failure and discouragement.

Pause for Reflection: Reflect on Your Own Fictional Finalism
Before moving on, take a moment to think about your own 'ideal self.' Write down an imagined future goal you've been chasing—perhaps something you believe will finally make you feel accomplished or worthy. How long have you been striving for this goal? How far away does it feel?

From Self-Criticism to Self-Support: A Case Study
Meet Jason.

Jason was a high achiever. He had a great job and solid career, but was also deeply afraid of failure.

Every time he made a mistake, his inner voice screamed:
- *"You should have done better!"*
- *"Why are you so behind?!"*
- *"If you fail, you're worthless!"*

No matter how much Jason accomplished, he never felt good enough. His inner criticism was louder than any external praise.

One day, in therapy, Jason was given a challenge:
"Write down everything your inner voice says to you. Now, imagine saying these things to a child. How does it feel?"

Jason was shocked.
- *"I would never speak to someone like this,"* he admitted.
- *"Why do I talk to myself this way?"*

That was the first step in rewriting his inner dialogue.
Jason began replacing self-criticism with self-support.

- Instead of saying, *"You're a failure,"* he said, *"You're learning, and that's okay."*
- Instead of saying, *"You should be better,"* he said, *"You are already enough."*

Over time, his inner critic softened, and his confidence grew.

What if you treated yourself with the same compassion you offer others?

Activity: The Self-Compassion Letter
Step 1: Write a letter to yourself as a friend would
- Imagine your best friend is struggling with self-doubt or perfectionism.
- Write them a kind, encouraging letter.
- Offer support, validation, and reassurance.

Step 2: Replace their name with your own
- Read the letter as if it were written to you.
- Notice how different it feels to receive kindness instead of criticism.

Step 3: Keep this letter & reread it when you need it
- Each time your inner critic speaks up, read this letter.
- Let it remind you that you deserve the same kindness you give others.

This simple but powerful exercise rewires the way you speak to yourself.

Exercise: The 'Flip the Script' Challenge
Next time you catch yourself thinking...
- *"I should have done better."* → Flip it to: *"I did my best with what I knew then."*
- *"I'm not good enough."* → Flip it to: *"I am enough, even if I'm still learning."*
- *"I need to be perfect."* → Flip it to: *"Done is better than perfect."*

Write down three negative thoughts you catch yourself saying. Flip them. Repeat them daily.

Bonus: How to Recover from Perfectionist Spirals
- **Catching Yourself:** Notice when your inner critic takes over—do you feel tense? Overwhelmed?
- **Step Back: Ask yourself,** *"Will this matter in a year? Or even in a week?"*
- **Reset the Standard:** Aim for progress, not perfection. Remind yourself: *"Excellence is not the same as flawlessness."*

Small Action: When you feel yourself slipping into a perfectionist spiral, say: *"I am allowed to be imperfect."*

Try This Practice: When your inner critic shows up this week, pause and ask: **"What would a loyal inner voice say to me right now?"** Write it down. Say it out loud. Let that voice grow stronger—one kind sentence at a time.

Pause for Reflection: What Would Your Inner Cheerleader Say?
- What kind statement can you start telling yourself daily?
- If your best friend had your struggles, how would you encourage them?
- What stops you from speaking to yourself with that kindness?
- Write down your answer and commit to shifting one negative thought this week.

Chapter Summary
For perfectionists, the inner critic is a familiar voice—loud, constant, and relentless. It disguises itself as motivation but often leaves behind shame, burnout, and the exhausting belief that nothing you do is ever enough.

In this chapter, we pulled back the curtain on that voice. We explored where it comes from, how childhood experiences and impossible standards shaped it, and—most importantly—how it can be rewritten. Through real stories and practical exercises, you learned that encouragement, not criticism, builds real growth. That kindness isn't weakness—it's the foundation of resilience.

You practiced replacing perfectionist pressure with self-compassion. You challenged fictional goals that kept joy just out of reach. And you met a new voice inside yourself—the inner cheerleader who doesn't need you to be flawless to believe in your worth.

Because when you stop chasing perfection and start offering yourself encouragement, everything begins to shift.

You become someone who can try without fear. Fail without shame. And live with more ease.

In Chapter 13, Dare to Be Imperfect, we'll take this self-compassion one step further.

Now that you've softened your inner voice, we'll explore how embracing imperfection isn't just okay—it's your greatest strength. You'll learn how to stop proving yourself and start trusting yourself. Because the life you want doesn't begin when you finally 'get it right'—it starts when you stop trying so hard to be someone you're not.

Let's step into wholeness—flaws, strengths, and all.

PART V: EMBRACE IMPERFECTION AND RESILIENCE

This is where transformation happens.

In Part V, we release the fear of failure, embrace imperfection, and step into self-acceptance. The goal is not to erase our perfectionist tendencies but to live with more freedom, resilience, and self-compassion than ever before.

Chapter 13: Dare to Be Imperfect — The courage to relinquish the need to always be in control.

Chapter 14: Failure as Your Greatest Teacher — Learning to see failure as essential to growth.

Chapter 15: The Art of Self-Acceptance — The final shift: from proving your worth to believing in it.

CHAPTER 13: DARE TO BE IMPERFECT

When achievement becomes the only measure of value, we lose sight of who we are beyond our roles.

In Adlerian psychology, significance is found not in superiority, but in belonging and usefulness.

We're taught that perfection is the path to approval. That if we just get it all right—our performance, our appearance, our timing—we'll finally feel worthy. But what if that's the very thing keeping us stuck?

We live in a world that rewards doing over being, where our worth feels tied to productivity, not presence. But what if a meaningful life isn't found in perfection, but in the moments we allow ourselves to simply be?

What If You Didn't Hide?
For most of your life, you've likely believed perfection is the only way to be accepted.
- *"If I get everything right, I'll be respected."*
- *"If I don't make mistakes, people will approve of me."*
- *"If I appear flawless, I won't be judged."*

But here's the truth:
- Perfection is exhausting.
- Perfection is an illusion.
- Perfection is not the key to love, success, or fulfillment.

So, what is?

The Willingness to Be Seen as Imperfect.

This chapter is about breaking free from the fear of imperfection and realizing that it is not a flaw—it is your greatest asset.

Breaking free from the fear of imperfection is the first step—but what does that look like? Alfred Adler believed the key was not just accepting imperfection but having the courage to embrace it fully. As Adlerian psychologist Rudolf Dreikurs put it, one of the most powerful steps we can take is to develop the 'courage to be imperfect.' It's not a flaw to be embraced reluctantly, but a cornerstone of mental health and connection.

The Courage to Be Imperfect

The topic of courage must be one of my favorite Adlerian concepts. Adler taught us about the 'courage to be imperfect.' Perfectionism traps us in fear- fear of making mistakes, fear of judgment. But how exactly do we embrace our imperfections? As Brene Brown says in her book *The Gifts of Imperfection*, *"The way we gain courage is by couraging."* To me, being courageous is moving forward with something that you really want, even though it may be scary or unknown. Another favorite definition is credited to a fellow Adlerian, Lindsay Hill, who says courage is *"your willingness and the number of actions you're willing to take to move to face life's challenges."* Adler might say courage is the ability to confront and overcome feelings of inferiority or inadequacy. This can include facing challenges and striving for personal growth despite obstacles such as fear of the unknown or anxiety.

Think back to a time in your life when you were courageous. Reflect on how it felt- what were the challenges and gains?

Many clients who struggle with perfectionism complain of struggling to be 'in the moment and present' and their authentic selves. There is courage and vulnerability in shifting our focus from being 'perfect' to being 'real' and 'authentic.' Imperfection isn't a rebellion against standards, it's a return to yourself. It invites us into life, not out of it.

How can moving away from perfectionism and embracing imperfection change your life? Think about the freedom it could bring, the energy you'd save, and how it could deepen your connection with others.

Permitting ourselves to be imperfect unlocks a new level of self-acceptance and connection. Now, let's explore practical exercises that help build this mindset in everyday life.

Adler taught us about the 'courage to be imperfect.' Perfectionism traps us in fear—fear of making mistakes and fear of judgment. But embracing our imperfections is where actual growth and happiness lie. It's about shifting our focus from being 'perfect' to becoming 'real' and 'authentic.'

The courage to be imperfect isn't just about accepting flaws; it's about embracing the power of imperfect action. Perfectionism often leads to procrastination and missed opportunities. We become paralyzed by the fear of not being good enough, so we never even start.

The Science Behind Embracing Imperfection
Studies in positive psychology show that embracing imperfection reduces stress and increases resilience.
- Dr. Kristin Neff's research on self-compassion reveals that people who accept their flaws experience less anxiety and greater motivation.
- The irony? Fear of imperfection paralyzes us, while accepting it frees us to improve and grow.
- The goal is not to eliminate mistakes—it's to learn to fail forward.

Reflection:
How has fearing imperfection held you back? What could change if you embraced it instead?

The Perfectionist's Fear: Being Seen as Flawed
- Have you ever held back from speaking up because you feared saying the wrong thing?
- Do you avoid situations where you might not perform perfectly?

For perfectionists, imperfection is not just uncomfortable—it feels like a threat.
- The fear isn't just about making mistakes—it's about how others perceive us.
- The belief is that if we are flawed, we will be judged, rejected, or exposed as 'not good enough.'

Perfectionism as a Defense Mechanism
But at its core, perfectionism isn't just about high standards—it's about control.

- Perfectionism is often a way to protect ourselves from vulnerability.
- We think we can avoid criticism, embarrassment, or failure if we appear flawless.
- If we always do things perfectly, we believe we can control how people see us.

But the irony? Perfectionism doesn't make us more accepted—it makes us more disconnected.

People are drawn to authenticity, not perfection.

What if you allowed yourself to be honest instead of striving for perfection?

Case Study: The Fear of Looking 'Unprepared'
Meet David.

He was known as 'the expert' in his workplace. He prided himself on always having the answers.

But this meant he never admitted when unsure, even if it meant pretending to know more than he did.
- The turning point? A colleague once said, *"I admire how you always seem to have the answers."* Instead of feeling proud, David felt trapped.
- He realized he wasn't growing—he was hiding behind perfection.

One day, he challenged himself: Instead of faking certainty, he said, *"I don't know, but I'll find out."*
- The result? No one judged him. Instead, they respected his honesty.
- By daring to be imperfect, he gained more trust and credibility, not less.

Lesson: People respect authenticity more than perfection.

Pause for Reflection: Why Do We Admire Imperfect People?

Think about the people you admire most.
1. Are they flawless or real, open, and imperfect?
2. Do you connect more with someone who shares their struggles, or someone who hides behind perfection?
3. What does this reveal about how you perceive your imperfections?

Write down your thoughts. Could embracing your imperfections make you more relatable, not less?

The Freedom of Imperfection: A Real-Life Shift

Meet Rachel.

Rachel had spent years chasing perfection. She never spoke up unless she was 100% sure of her answer. She worked late nights, triple-checking every detail.

"I thought if I could just be perfect, I'd finally feel secure."

But then, Rachel's 'perfect' world came crashing down.

One day at work, she made a mistake on an important project. She was sure it would ruin her career. But instead of criticism, her manager said:

"Everyone makes mistakes, Rachel. What matters is what we do next."

- For the first time, she realized that imperfection wasn't a disaster—it was human.
- And instead of people rejecting her, they supported her.

"That moment changed everything. I realized I could stop trying to prove myself all the time. I could let people see the real me, and I wouldn't lose anything. I gained more than I ever had."

What if your greatest fear—being seen as imperfect—was your greatest source of freedom?

Pause for Reflection: What Are You Afraid of?
1. What situations make you most afraid of being seen as imperfect?
2. What do you believe would happen if people saw you fail?
3. Have you ever judged yourself more harshly than others judged you?

Write down your fears. Acknowledging them is the first step in dismantling them.

Bridging Fear and Action: The 'Acting As If' Technique

Understanding perfectionism's grip is one thing—actually changing our behavior is another. This is where many perfectionists get stuck. They intellectually understand that embracing imperfection is important, but the fear still holds them back emotionally.

One powerful Adlerian approach we use with clients is the 'Acting As If' technique. This behavioral experiment helps interrupt the rigid, fear-based thinking that perfectionism creates. It's a way to test new beliefs in real life, rather than waiting to feel ready.

Here's how we guide clients through it:

For one week, choose one specific area where perfectionism holds you back—maybe it's sending emails at work, contributing to group discussions, or sharing something creative. Then, deliberately act as if you already have the mindset you want to build.

We once worked with a surgeon who struggled with impostor syndrome. She agreed to 'act as if' she belonged at the table during hospital board meetings. Instead of over-preparing and still doubting herself, she made a commitment to speak early in discussions, ask questions when unsure, and state her opinions without apologizing or qualifying her expertise.

"The first meeting was terrifying," she told us. *"I felt like a fraud pretending to be confident. But by the third meeting, something shifted. I realized my colleagues were treating me differently—with more respect—and I wasn't even thinking about whether I belonged anymore."*

The brilliance of this technique is that it flips the perfectionist script. Rather than saying, *"I'll feel confident when I'm perfect,"* it invites you to try, *"I'll act as if I'm already enough—and let the feeling follow."*

Try It Yourself:
1. Identify a situation where perfectionism limits you.
2. Define how someone with healthy self-acceptance would behave in that situation.
3. For one week, act as if you already had that mindset—even if it feels unnatural or awkward.
4. Document what happens, both in your behavior and in how others respond.
5. Reflect on any insights:
   - What surprised you?
   - What fears didn't come true?
   - What changed in how you see yourself?

This technique embodies Adler's belief that action often comes before emotional change. You don't need to feel confident to start behaving confidently, and you don't need to feel perfect to stop performing for approval. You can act as if you are already enough and watch what happens next.

Small Acts of Imperfection: Daily Practice
An Introduction to The Author's Personal Experiment With Imperfection.
For years, I tried to control everything. My schedule had to be planned perfectly, my work had to be flawless, and even my home had to be tidy at all times. I believed that letting things slip, even a little, meant I was failing.

Then I decided to try something different, allowing small acts of imperfection into my life. I sent an email without obsessively proofreading it. I left a small mess in my kitchen overnight. Instead of pretending I had all the answers, I allowed myself to answer *"I don't know"* in conversations.

And nothing terrible happened. The world didn't fall apart. I didn't become less worthy. Instead, I felt... free.

- Imperfection is a muscle—the more you practice it, the more comfortable it becomes.

What small act of imperfection could you allow today?

Quick Challenge: 'The Imperfect Action' Experiment
Challenge:
1. Pick one small area of life where perfectionism holds you back.
   - **Example:** Over-editing emails? Obsessing over small details? Avoiding trying new things?
2. Today, take ONE imperfect action.
   - Send the email with one typo.
   - Post something without overthinking.
   - Let yourself stumble over your words.

Then observe:
Did the world fall apart? Or did you feel freer?

The goal? To prove to yourself that imperfection doesn't make you less worthy—it makes you human.

Reframe Fear of Judgment: 'People Care Less Than You Think'
Harvard research on the 'Spotlight Effect' found that we overestimate how much people notice our flaws.
- Reality check: People are too busy thinking about themselves to judge every small mistake we make.
- You forgot what you were saying in a meeting? Most people won't remember.
- You stumbled over a word? No one cares as much as you think.

The lesson? You are already free—you must train yourself to believe it.

What's one 'mistake' you've obsessed over that others probably forgot?

Activity: The Imperfection Reframe
Step 1: Identify an imperfection you've been trying to hide
- What is something you try to fix, control, or mask because you're afraid of how it looks?
- **Example:** You may struggle speaking confidently in meetings, so you stay silent.

Step 2: Reframe it as something that brings value
- Instead of seeing it as a weakness, consider: What is its hidden strength?
- **Example:** Your struggle speaking up may make you a better listener.

Step 3: Accept it as part of your human experience
- Ask yourself: Would you judge a friend for this same imperfection?
- How would your life change if you embraced this instead of hiding it?

Imperfection is not something to be ashamed of—it is a source of connection, growth, and authenticity.

Pause for Reflection: What If Imperfection Were Strength?
1. Think of someone you admire—do they have imperfections?
2. What makes them inspiring? Their perfection or their ability to embrace flaws?
3. What would happen if you permitted yourself to be imperfect?

Write down how embracing imperfection could change your life.

Chapter Summary
This chapter was a permission slip—a deep exhale, a quiet rebellion against the lie that perfection equals worth.

We looked at the cost of flawless living—the pressure, the hiding, the endless performance—and made space for something far more liberating: authenticity. You saw how perfectionism isn't just about high standards; it's about fear—fear of judgment, fear of being seen, fear of not being enough.

But as you explored through real stories and daily practices, you discovered that imperfection doesn't push people away—it draws them closer. You don't have to prove your value by being spotless. Your humanness is your greatest strength.

You learned that:
- People respect honesty more than polish.
- Confidence grows through action, not waiting to feel "ready."
- Small acts of imperfection build self-trust, courage, and freedom.

As you move forward, keep asking: What would it look like to stop performing and start showing up?

In the next chapter, we'll take this one step further. Because the thing many perfectionists still fear—maybe more than anything else—is failure.

But what if failure wasn't a dead end?

What if it were your greatest teacher?

In Chapter 14: Failure as Your Greatest Teacher, we'll explore how the moments we dread the most can become the foundations for confidence, resilience, and real success.

Let's walk toward failure—and find power in the stumble.

CHAPTER 14: FAILURE AS YOUR GREATEST TEACHER

You were never meant to be perfect. You were meant to be whole.

Adler emphasized the unity of the self, not flawless performance, but integrated living.

You feel the heat rising in your face. Your heart pounds. The weight of judgment—yours and everyone else's—settles on your chest. You failed. And for a perfectionist, failure isn't just something that happened—it's proof that you are not enough.

The Failure That Changed Everything
At some point in your life, you've failed.
- Maybe you missed an opportunity you wanted.
- Maybe you made a mistake in front of others.
- Maybe you tried something new, and it didn't work.

And if you're a perfectionist, that failure felt unbearable.

For perfectionists, failure is not just about making mistakes; it's about identity.
- *"If I fail, what does that say about me?"*
- *"Does failure mean I'm not good enough?"*
- *"Will people see me differently if I don't succeed?"*

But what if failure wasn't a mark of shame? What if failure were your greatest teacher?

Adlerian Insight: Alfred Adler viewed failure not as a flaw, but as feedback. For Adler, all human striving happens within a social context, meaning that mistakes aren't personal verdicts — they're information. Failure is simply part of the path toward growth and contribution.

This chapter is about shifting your relationship with failure from avoidance and fear to growth and resilience.

For perfectionists, mistakes often feel like proof of inadequacy rather than stepping stones toward improvement. But what if mistakes weren't signs of failure at all? What if they were simply part of learning and growth? If we can reframe how we view challenges, we can shift from self-criticism to self-acceptance.

If we can reframe how we view challenges, we can be less self-critical and more encouraged to move forward with life's tasks. Facing challenges with resilience and openness to learning can lead to significant personal growth. Challenges are not threats to perfection but opportunities to learn more about oneself and evolve. Perfectionists may prefer to do things they know they do well and are familiar with. Thinking about a challenge and 'uncharted territory' can feel overwhelming and scary.

How do you feel about mistakes? What happens when you make a mistake? What do you usually tell yourself? What would it feel like to have a healthy attitude towards mistakes? Rather than seeing mistakes as a failure, Adler believed mistakes are an inevitable aspect of life and learning. Instead of dwelling on past mistakes or fearing future missteps, Adlerians advocate for a forward-thinking approach that focuses on learning from experiences instead of self-criticism and avoiding trying in the future. Ideally, mistakes would not be associated with self-worth. Self-worth should be solid and consistent, which can be recognized and accepted based on your innate value, regardless of performance.

When you reflect on something you did, or a choice, and consider it a mistake, you analyze it from a new, more enlightened perspective that you would not have had without the error. For example, when children learn to walk, they know how to balance by falling. If the child fell, then sat down and thought about what a clutz they were and how embarrassed they were about falling or even go so far as to say, *'I'm a failure and might as well just keep crawling since I can't seem to figure out this walking thing'*, they'd never start walking! It's natural for the child to get back up, try again, and fall repeatedly until they begin to master walking. The idea we are trying to convey is as simple as this: if the child didn't fall, they would not learn to balance.

Story Spotlight: Anna's Startup

Anna spent years building her small business. When her first big launch failed, she spiraled, believing the failure confirmed her deepest fear: *"I'm not cut out for this."* But looking back, Anna now calls that moment her best teacher. *"That failure showed me where I wasn't asking for help. It taught me to collaborate, to adjust, and most importantly, to believe that mistakes didn't make me less worthy — they made me more prepared."*

Failure didn't end her business — it strengthened it.

Some questions you could ask yourself after making a mistake are, *"What did this experience teach me about what I want?" "How can what I learn help me to live a better life?"* Perfectionists tend to believe that criticizing themselves and putting themselves down for their mistakes will help them improve. Failure teaches us something perfectionism never can: humility and connection. When we allow ourselves to fail, we soften the walls we build around our worth and let others in — not because we're flawless, but because we're human.

In reality, embracing the error allows you to have an expanded perspective and analyze its positives and negatives. Embracing mistakes is not the same thing as condoning them. Mistakes lead us closer to success, particularly when we embrace and accept them.

By shifting our perspective on mistakes, we move from avoiding failure to embracing growth. Mistakes do not reflect our worth, they are opportunities to adjust, adapt, and build resilience. The next step is learning practical ways to apply this mindset daily.

Pause for Reflection

Think back to the last time you made a mistake. Maybe it was at work, home, or a conversation with someone important to you. How did it make you feel? What were the thoughts that came up?

Many of us find it hard to accept mistakes. There are both physical and psychological reasons behind this.

Many perfectionists don't just fear failure—they feel it intensely, both emotionally and physically. Science backs this up: the brain processes failure in the same way it processes physical pain, which explains why making mistakes can feel so overwhelming.

Our Body's Response

When we fail, our body reacts as if we're in physical pain. The same areas of the brain that process physical pain are triggered when we experience emotional discomfort, such as shame. So, when we make a mistake, we feel it emotionally and physically. Mistakes can feel deeply uncomfortable, as if something is wrong with us for not getting it right.

Shame is one of the most painful emotions we can feel, and many people will go to great lengths to avoid it. But here's the truth: mistakes don't have to result in shame. By viewing mistakes as a normal and necessary part of learning, we take away their power to make us feel unworthy. Instead of seeing mistakes as proof that something is wrong with us, we can begin to see them as opportunities for growth and self-discovery.

Many of us have grown up in environments where we were sheltered from failure, leaving us unprepared for life's challenges. Some people have even been described as 'failure deprived,' meaning they never learned how to cope with mistakes because they were protected from them for so long. When failure finally comes, it can feel overwhelming, even paralyzing. But here's the thing: pain isn't the enemy—it's a teacher.

The first step is to reflect on your relationship with failure. Do you feel the need to avoid it at all costs? Is there an underlying fear that making mistakes makes you less capable and less worthy? These beliefs can hold us back. When we stop avoiding failure and start seeing it as a path to growth, we open ourselves up to new possibilities and greater resilience.

When you face a mistake or setback, lean into it. Acknowledge the discomfort and remind yourself, *"This is hard, but it's also an opportunity for growth."*

Now that we understand why failure feels so painful, the next step is learning how to create space for mistakes in our lives. Instead of avoiding failure, we can build resilience by shifting how we approach and learn from our setbacks.

Create Space for Learning and Growth

It's also important to examine how you handle your own mistakes. How often do you allow yourself to make them, and what messages do you tell yourself when you do? Practice slowing down and recognizing the importance of mistakes in your life.

Say things like, *"This is tough, and it's going to take time and effort before I get it right."*

You might also want to reflect on your past experiences. Look back at moments when things didn't go as planned. What did you learn from those situations? How did they help you grow into the person you are today? These reflections help build a growth mindset and remind you that your journey matters far more than any result.

One way to engage with this mindset is to make it a habit to ask yourself, *"What's my oops for today?"* Please take a moment to acknowledge something that didn't go perfectly, and lean into the discomfort instead of trying to avoid it.

Don't rush to fix or solve it immediately when reflecting on it. Instead, consider how it felt, why it happened, and what you can learn from it.

When you embrace mistakes and view them as part of your path to personal growth, you cultivate resilience, self-compassion, and the courage to continue moving forward, imperfect but constantly evolving. We said it once before, and we will say it again: you're human, and that means inherently being perfectly imperfect.

Anxiety about the future often revolves around the fear that we will be unable to 'handle' what could happen, possible mistakes, and the 'unknown.' When we look at our strengths and the things we have accomplished and overcome, we can use those as evidence that we can deal with whatever life brings us.

It's natural for people to worry about making mistakes, as mistakes are often associated with negative consequences or feelings of failure and shame. However, many fail to recognize that mistakes are essential to learning and can contribute significantly to personal growth and skill development. Mistakes provide valuable feedback that helps us understand what went wrong and how to improve. Each mistake offers an opportunity to learn and refine one's approach, leading to greater proficiency and mastery. Some of the most significant advancements in history have resulted from mistakes or failures that spurred innovation and creativity. Furthermore, making mistakes generates resilience and perseverance. When individuals encounter setbacks or failures, they are presented with a choice: to give up or to persist despite the challenges.

Those who embrace their mistakes as learning opportunities tend to develop a growth mindset, viewing setbacks as temporary obstacles that can be overcome with effort and determination. Additionally, mistakes often lead to unexpected discoveries and insights. By pushing boundaries and experimenting with different approaches, individuals may stumble upon new ideas or solutions they wouldn't have otherwise considered. 'Mistakes are signs of incompetence or failure, but rather stepping stones to success.'

Mistakes are not roadblocks; they are stepping stones toward growth and mastery. By shifting our mindset from fearing mistakes to embracing them, we allow ourselves to keep learning, evolving, and moving forward confidently. The following section will explore how to take actionable steps toward applying this mindset in everyday life.

The Failure That Defined Me (Until It Didn't)
A personal story from the author.

There was a time when failure felt like the worst thing that could happen to me. I had worked tirelessly on a project I believed in—poured my heart and soul into it. And then, it flopped—not just a tiny mistake—a full-blown, public, embarrassing failure.

- I remember standing there, feeling exposed. My mind raced with thoughts like, *'Everyone will think I'm a fraud.' 'This is proof I'm not good enough.' 'I'll never recover from this.'*
- What hurt the most wasn't the failure itself—it was what I told myself about it.

Looking back, failure didn't break me. It gave me clarity. It forced me to ask why I believe failure is a measure of my worth.

- That was when I realized failure is only permanent if you stop trying. The most successful, resilient people aren't those who avoid failure—they are the ones who use it as fuel.

I had spent my life trying to avoid failure. But what if failure was the very thing that would teach me how to succeed?

Why Failure Feels Like a Threat to Perfectionists
Have you ever gone out of your way to avoid failure?
- Maybe you procrastinate on big goals because you fear messing up.
- Maybe you play it safe rather than risk looking foolish.
- Maybe you judge yourself harshly for even the smallest mistakes.

For perfectionists, failure isn't just a setback—it feels like an attack on their self-worth.
- We've been taught that failure = incompetence.
- We believe mistakes mean we're falling behind.
- We think if we fail, people will judge us.

Society's Conditioning of Failure
But where does this fear of failure come from?
- As children, we are naturally curious. We try, fail, adjust, and try again—without shame.
- But as we grow up, we are taught that failure is embarrassing.
- Schools, workplaces, and even social media reinforce the idea that mistakes mean weakness.

But what if failure was not something to fear but something to embrace?

Every great innovation, breakthrough, or success has been built on failure.
- Edison failed 1,000 times before creating the lightbulb.
- Oprah was told she wasn't 'fit for television.'
- J.K. Rowling's Harry Potter manuscript was rejected 12 times.

The difference? They didn't let failure define them—they let it refine them.

What if you started seeing failure as feedback, not as a failure? Perfectionists often struggle with failure because they see it as evidence that they are 'not enough' rather than a stepping stone toward mastery. But what if we shifted our perspective? Instead of believing we must already 'be' successful, we could see ourselves as always 'becoming', constantly growing, improving, and evolving. This shift can help us redefine failure as essential to personal development. Let's explore this further with the concept of 'Being vs. Becoming.

From 'Being' to 'Becoming'

The concept of 'being versus becoming,' introduced by Lydia Sicher, offers insight into feelings of inferiority compared to an inferiority complex. To 'be' reflects the desire or pressure to instantly embody an ideal or role, like a successful business owner, without genuinely acknowledging the time, experience, and growth required to fulfill that role. Essentially, it involves a need to achieve the final goal without going through the necessary process or feeling discouraged early on if it feels tedious. For instance, I would love to 'be' a ballet dancer (again with the ballerina goal!), but I know this would require significant time, effort, and dedication, with slow results. After just a few classes, I want to perform those twirls on pointed toes! The reality is that what you don't see from a seasoned ballet dancer is years of practice, training, dedication, and plenty of mistakes and injuries that brought them to the state of 'being.'

To 'become,' on the other hand, means acknowledging and committing to the journey toward a goal, understanding that learning and development are continuous processes. It involves gradually building toward an aspirational state through deliberate effort and persistence. For the ballet dancer, this means starting with an introductory class and continuing on this journey, no matter how long it takes to reach their goals, despite any struggles or setbacks. We often don't see that progress immediately when we progress toward our goals. But looking back, we can see how each small step contributed to our current position. It's like building a house; the foundation must be laid before the roof and windows go on.

Activity: Reframe Immediate Desires into Growth Journeys
Step 1: Immediate Desires vs. Long-Term Goals
- List out immediate desires related to your personal or professional life—the things you think you need to 'be' right now (e.g., *"be successful," "be perfect," "be admired"*).
- Next to each, articulate what the journey to achieving these desires might look like.
- What does it mean to 'become' successful, compassionate, or resilient?

Step 2: Identifying steps
- For each 'become' journey, break down the process into smaller, achievable steps.
- Reflect on the learning, experiences, and milestones each step will involve.

Step 3: Reflection
- Reflect on how shifting from a 'be' to a 'become' mindset changes your feelings toward these goals.
- Does it reduce pressure?
- Does it empower you to act?

Key takeaway: Growth is not about arriving at a perfect destination—it's about embracing the process of transformation.

Activity: Celebrate the 'Becoming' Process
Objective:
Recognize progress and learning as achievements, which will help you cultivate a growth-oriented mindset.

Step 1: Journey Log
- Begin a Journey Log where you document your 'becoming' journey toward a significant goal.
- Include challenges faced, lessons learned, and small victories.

Step 2: Growth Milestones
- Identify and celebrate each step of progress, no matter how small.
- Acknowledge new skills learned, fears overcome, or insights gained.
- **Action Tip:** Reward yourself with a small treat or a moment of relaxation for each milestone reached.

Step 3: Peer Sharing
- If comfortable, share your journey with a trusted friend or peer.
- Sharing can provide additional perspectives, support, and validation of your growth.
- Consider creating a support group or partnering with someone on a similar path for mutual encouragement.

Key takeaway: Every step forward is progress, even if it feels small. Celebrate the journey, not just the destination.

Activity to Focus on the 'Become'

Perfectionism often fixates on an ideal state of being—what we think we must 'be' to be valued, successful, or loved. This activity shifts the focus from immediate attainment to the ongoing journey of 'becoming,' helping you appreciate growth as a continual, rewarding process.

Pause for Reflection: The Power of 'Becoming'

Growth is not about arriving at a perfect destination but about embracing transformation. Each step you take toward 'becoming' is a testament to your resilience, courage, and commitment to living authentically.

Activity: What If You Learned Like a Child?

- Think about how young children learn.
- When they learn to walk, they fall hundreds of times—yet they don't see it as failure.
- When they learn to talk, they mispronounce words but don't feel shame.
- They don't quit, they don't overthink, they don't fear looking 'stupid'—they try again.

When did you stop giving yourself that same grace?

Step 1: Identify a risk you're avoiding
- What is something you are afraid to try because you might fail?
- Is it learning a new skill, speaking up, taking on a leadership role, or expressing yourself creatively?

Step 2: Shift your mindset to experimentation
- Instead of seeing it as a pass/fail test, think:
- What can I learn from this?
- How would a child approach this challenge?

Step 3: Fail forward challenge
- Pick one thing to try this week—even if you do it poorly.
- Give yourself permission to fail and observe what happens.
- Write down what you learned from trying, not just succeeding.

Key takeaway: Your willingness to fail is what makes you grow.

From Shame to Strength: A Real-Life Failure Story
Meet James.

James was a high achiever who always played it safe. He avoided risks because he feared failing publicly.

Then, one day, he failed big.

He pitched a project at work that ultimately flopped. His ideas were rejected, and he felt humiliated in front of his team.
- He spent weeks replaying the moment in his head.
- He told himself he had ruined his career.
- He almost quit his job out of shame.

But then something changed.

One day, his mentor said something that stuck with him:
"If you never fail, you're not pushing yourself hard enough."

James realized something:
- Every successful person he admired had failed many times.
- Failure wasn't a sign of incompetence—it was proof he was trying something bold.

Instead of quitting, James did something radical—he started seeing failure as feedback.
- He looked at what went wrong without self-blame.
- He took the lessons learned and applied them to his next project.
- Instead of shrinking, he grew.

Failure did not break him—it built him.

What if failure wasn't the end of the story, but the beginning of your growth?

Activity: Mining Gold from the Rubble

Think about a failure that still stings when you remember it. Maybe it was public, like bombing a presentation, or private, like giving up on a personal goal. What emotions does this memory trigger?

Now shift perspective. Was there anything valuable that emerged from this experience? Sometimes the lessons aren't immediately obvious—they might have shown up weeks or months later as a changed perspective or a new direction.

Try reimagining this story not as a chapter called "My Failure" but as "The Turn." What title would you give this experience now, looking back with the wisdom you've gained?

Chapter Summary

This chapter was a reintroduction to failure, not as something to fear, but as something to welcome.

You may have seen mistakes as proof that you weren't enough for years. A failed project, a missed opportunity, a misstep in front of others felt like a judgment, a scarlet letter on your worth. But today, you started rewriting that story.

We explored how perfectionism ties your value to flawless performance, and how freeing it is to untie that knot. You learned that:
- Failure is not a flaw in your character; it's a growth feature.
- Your brain might panic when things go wrong, but your worth is never up for debate.
- Every misstep contains a message, a shift, a turning point if you choose to look closer.

You heard stories of people who fell and got back up stronger, not despite failure but because of it. You were invited to experiment with failing forward, to challenge yourself not to avoid mistakes but to mine them for gold.

You don't need to 'be' perfect to grow—you need to *keep becoming*.

In the next and final chapter, we'll tie it all together. Because the greatest lesson of all isn't how to fix yourself—it's how to accept yourself finally.

What if you stopped chasing an ideal... and started embracing the truth of who you already are?

Let's take that final, freeing step—into Chapter 15, The Art of Self-Acceptance.

CHAPTER 15: THE ART OF SELF-ACCEPTANCE

Real success isn't found in applause but in alignment.

The Adlerian path invites us to succeed by contributing, connecting, and showing up with courage.

The Chase for Enoughness

Have you ever felt like no matter what you achieve, it's never enough?
- You reach a goal, but instead of celebrating, you set the next one.
- You get validation from others, but it only lasts a moment.
- You always feel like there's more you need to do, be, or prove.

This is the perfectionist's trap—the endless chase for enoughness.

But what if the problem isn't that you're not enough? What if the problem is the belief that you have to earn your worth?

This chapter is about stepping off the hamster wheel and realizing that you are already enough.

Adlerian Insight: Alfred Adler taught that self-worth is never earned—it's inherent. His work reminds us that social usefulness, connection, and contribution ground our sense of belonging. You don't need perfection to matter. You matter because you're part of the world, not because of your performance.

Why You've Never Felt Like You're Enough

Why is it that no matter how much you accomplish, you still feel like you should be doing more?

Perfectionists believe their worth is tied to achievement.
- *"I'll be enough when I get that promotion."*
- *"I'll feel worthy when I lose weight."*
- *"I'll be happy when I accomplish more."*

But the truth is, you've been moving the finish line your entire life.
- You never let yourself feel like enough because you keep raising the bar.
- No achievement ever feels permanent, because you always think there's another level you must reach.

But what if your worth was never meant to be something you had to prove?

What if you were enough all along?

Pause for Reflection: Where Are You Seeking Enoughness?
1. What areas of your life make you feel you must prove yourself?
2. Where do you believe you must achieve more to be 'enough'?
3. What would change if you believed your worth was unconditional?

Write down your thoughts. Recognizing the cycle of seeking validation is the first step to breaking free.

The Moment I Knew I Was Enough
A Personal Story From The Author

For years, I lived by the idea that if I just did more—worked harder, achieved more, met every expectation—I would finally feel like I was enough.

I thought the next accomplishment would bring peace, but it never did. No matter what I achieved, my mind always found the next thing I should strive for.

Then, one day, everything changed. I sat alone after a long day, exhausted from chasing another goal. And for the first time, I asked myself: *'What if I didn't need to do anything to be enough? What if I just... was?'*

At first, the thought felt unnatural. But the more I sat with it, the more I realized that I had spent my entire life trying to prove something that was never in question. I had always been enough—I had never let myself believe it.

That was the first time I truly felt free.

What would happen if you permitted yourself to feel enough, right now?

Redefine Success: A Real-Life Transformation
Meet Sophia.

Sophia was a high achiever who built her self-worth around external validation.

She thought if she worked harder, impressed more people, and hit every milestone, she would finally feel satisfied.
- But the promotions, praise, and achievements never lasted.
- Every success only created more pressure to maintain an impossible standard.

"It felt like I was constantly running, but I never arrived."

Then, something shifted.

"One day, I asked myself: Would I still be enough if I never accomplished another thing?"
- That question terrified her.
- Because deep down, she believed she only mattered if she was achieving.
- But slowly, she realized her worth had never been about what she did—it was about who she was.

She stopped defining herself by her productivity.
- She started valuing rest, joy, and simply being present.
- And for the first time in her life, she felt whole.

Self-worth isn't about achievement. It's about connection. You are enough, not when you've earned it, but simply because you belong. What if success wasn't about doing more but believing you are already enough?

Activity: The Enough Exercise – Find Worth Within
Step 1: Identify where you seek external validation
- What areas of your life make you feel you must earn your worth?
- **Example:** Career, appearance, relationships, achievements.

Step 2: If these disappeared, would you still be enough?
- If your job, accomplishments, or external praise were gone, what would remain?
- What qualities make you valuable beyond what you achieve?

Step 3: Write a new definition of worth
- Instead of *"I am enough because I succeed,"* try *"I am enough because I exist."*
- Shift from conditional to unconditional self-worth.

Your worth was never meant to be earned—it is yours by default.

Key Takeaways
The paradox of perfectionism is that while we're busy constructing elaborate scaffolding of achievements to prove our worth, we miss the foundation that was always there. It's like spending a lifetime earning money to buy what you already own.

Most perfectionists I've worked with describe the same unsettling pattern: the goalposts never stay put. The promotion that was supposed to make everything okay reveals the next mountain to climb. The finish line keeps rolling backward just as you approach it.

For years, I thought my value depended on how much I could achieve, prove, and be.

If I worked hard, did everything right, and became perfect enough, I would finally feel worthy.

But no matter how much I accomplished, that feeling of 'enoughness' never came.

Until I stopped searching for it.

That was the moment I realized:
- I had been enough all along.
- I just never permitted myself to believe it.

Imperfection invites us into life, not out of it. The moment you stop chasing worth and start choosing connection, you step into the life that was waiting for you all along.

*You are not valuable because of what you do.
*You are valuable because of who you are.

And that has always been enough.

So, if you're still running, trying to prove yourself, trying to chase perfection, we want you to know something:
- You don't have to run anymore.
- You don't have to prove a single thing.
- You were already whole before you even started.

The Final Takeaway: The Freedom to Just Be

You've spent a long time running—chasing the next goal, the subsequent approval, the next moment where you could finally breathe and say, *"Now I'm enough."*

But that moment never came.

In this chapter, you stepped off that treadmill. You paused. You looked around. And for the first time, you asked: *What if I was already enough—even before the next win, the next checkbox, the next round of applause?*

We explored how perfectionism tricks you into tying your worth to performance, moves the finish line every time you get close, and keeps you striving for a version of yourself that doesn't even exist.

You heard stories of people who redefined success—not by doing more, but by believing differently.

You practiced what it means to root your worth in presence, not performance. To write a new story where your value isn't earned—it's remembered.
And maybe, just maybe, you felt a little exhale of relief.
Because deep down, you've always known:
- You're not here to be perfect.
- You're not here to prove anything.
- You're here to be you, and that's more than enough.

You matter, not when you're perfect, but when you're connected. The more you choose belonging over performance, the more your life expands.

What's Next?

This may be the end of the book, but it's the beginning of something bigger: a life that isn't built on proving, performing, or perfecting.

This is the moment you return home to yourself.

If this journey resonated with you, consider continuing it with our companion journal, designed to help you practice imperfection, self-kindness, and belonging, day by day.

Welcome back.

LIVING WELL WITH PERFECTIONISM

REFERENCES

Adler, A. (1956). *The Individual Psychology of Alfred Adler* (H. L. Ansbacher & R. R. Ansbacher, Eds.). Harper & Row.

Kfir, N. (2011). *Personality and Priorities: A Typology*. AuthorHouse.

Dreikurs, R. (1972). *Children: The Challenge*. Hawthorn Books.

LIVING WELL WITH PERFECTIONISM

ABOUT THE AUTHORS

Caroline Faifman

Caroline is a Licensed Mental Health Counselor and certified Adlerian psychotherapist. She has been in the mental health and wellness field for the last 20 years, starting as a yoga and mindfulness teacher. Caroline has a private practice in the Tampa Bay area. Most importantly, Caroline is a wife and mother to four incredible children.

Lindsay M. Turner

Lindsay is a Licensed Mental Health Counselor, coach, and founder of Reimagine Your Life, a boutique therapy and coaching practice based in

Boca Raton, Florida. She blends evidence-based therapy with creativity, personal style, and a hefty dose of real-life experience to help individuals move through life's transitions, quiet the noise of perfectionism, and reconnect with who they truly are.

Before entering the world of mental health, Lindsay built a successful career in hospitality, sales, and event planning—until she realized that, despite 'having it all together' on the outside, something inside her was longing for more. It was through her own experience with grief, heartbreak, and trauma that she knew it was time to make a change. That healing journey sparked her passion for helping others do the same.

Lindsay is trained in Cognitive Behavioral Therapy (CBT), Dialectical Behavior Therapy (DBT), Acceptance and Commitment Therapy (ACT), and Adlerian therapy. She is a member of the North American Society of Adlerian Psychology (NASAP). In her personal journey and professional work, she believes that true transformation begins from the inside out.

When she's not working with clients, you can find her soaking up the Florida sunshine, hosting impromptu dance parties in her living room, or making new memories with her greatest joy—her daughter, Raegan.

www.ingramcontent.com/pod-product-compliance
Lightning Source LLC
Chambersburg PA
CBHW070536090426
42735CB00013B/2997